SCULPTURE
WITH SIMPLE MATERIALS

By the Sunset Editorial Staff
with Robert and Joan Dawson

Lane Books · Menlo Park, California

PHOTOGRAPHS

Tom Burns, Jr.: page 94 (top right). Robert Cox: pages 6, 11, 12, 13, 17, 22, 23, 30, 33 (bottom), 35, 36 (top), 37 (bottom), 38 (bottom), 39 (center, bottom), 40, 50 (bottom), 52, 59 (top), 60, 64, 67, 68, 78, 80, 82, 84, 86, 90. Robert Dawson: pages 4, 10, 15, 20, 21, 26 (top, center, bottom left), 28 (left), 29 (left), 32, 33 (top), 36 (bottom), 37 (top), 38 (top), 39 (top), 41, 42, 45, 46, 47, 48, 49, 50 (top), 53, 55, 56, 58, 59 (bottom), 62, 63, 65, 66, 69, 75, 76, 79, 83, 85, 88. Jeannette Grossman: page 95 (top left). Art Hupy: page 94 (bottom left). Harry Marks: cover; pages 14, 18, 24, 26 (bottom right), 27, 28 (right), 29 (right), 44, 51, 54, 57, 70, 72, 74, 77, 89. Katherine L. Robertson: page 95 (top right). Darrow M. Watt: page 94 (top left, bottom right), 95 (bottom left, bottom right).

All drawings are by Joan Dawson.

Head and small totem shown on cover, courtesy of the Pacific Academy of the Arts. Sculptures shown on cover: child's head, clay; small totem, plaster and vermiculite; figure of a girl, plaster; colorful bird, papier mache. Projects on page 94 by William J. Shelley (top left), Howard J. Burnham (top right), Del MacBride (bottom left), Bella Feldman (bottom right). Projects on page 95 by Mrs. E. S. Beach, (top left), Jerry Kirwin (top right), Jack Millick (bottom left), William Shelley (bottom right).

CONTENTS

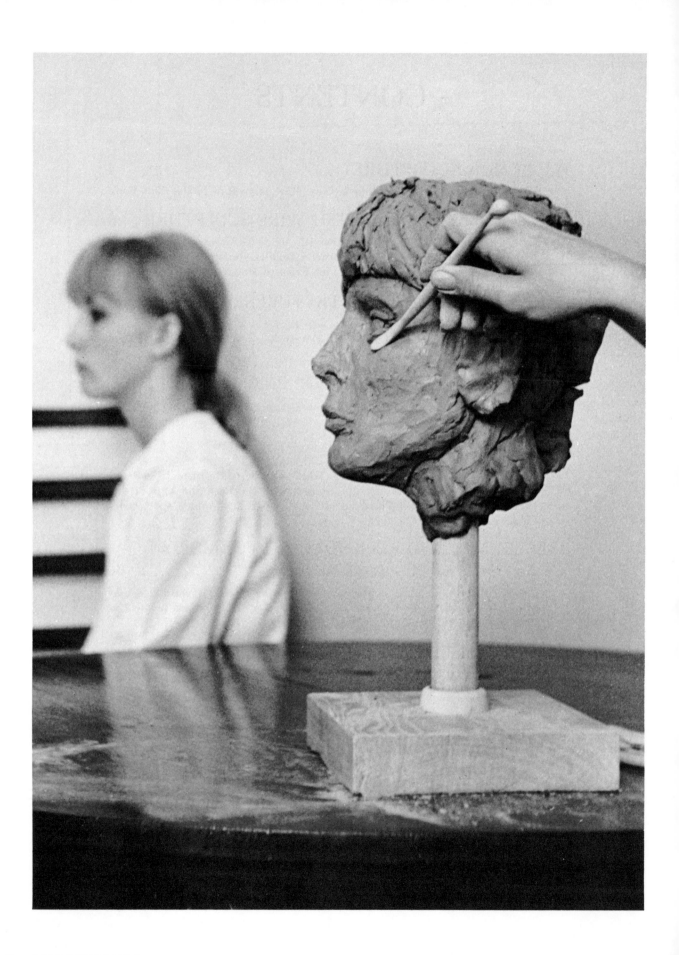

WHAT IS A SCULPTURE?

A sculpture is a modeled, three-dimensional form, created by man, which appeals to the eye. By this definition, a candlestick could be a sculpture; by tradition, a line is drawn between the useful and the artistic, and the word sculpture is reserved for objects created purely to stimulate the senses and the mind.

The artistic qualities of modern sculpture are very much the same as the artistic qualities of any age. However, there have been two major changes in the craft of sculpture which make it more available to the average man as an art to be enjoyed or practiced.

ALL ART IS ABSTRACT

Influenced strongly by simple, primitive forms, modern sculptors have turned away from the formal realism of Renaissance and Baroque sculpture to the art of abstracting. Abstract art is usually taken to mean art that does not represent any object itself. Nonetheless, abstraction has many meanings, and all art is essentially abstract. For example, a statue of a man on a horse, no matter how realistic, is nothing but a composed shape that tricks the imagination into thinking of a familiar object. You may be sure that the artist has simplified, rearranged, and distorted the actual shape of his model to accomplish this trick of realism. However, a modern sculptor would not want the viewer to concentrate entirely on the fact that such a shape is a rider, or the sculpture would not be seen as sculpture at all.

THE CHANGE TO NEW MATERIALS

By the invention of methods for working directly with everyday materials, such as wire, plaster, papier mache, and softwood lumber, modern sculpture has been freed from the mammoth workshops and long apprenticeships required for classical sculpting in marble or bronze. Each of these new materials has its own special qualities and limitations, which the sculptor tries to use to advantage. He lets his material express its own nature and determine its own craft.

While constantly experimenting with new materials, sculptors have also developed new styles and techniques of working with wood and stone, seeking to free artistic expression from hard labor and long years of academic study.

HOW TO USE THIS BOOK

This book is organized to teach design skills and craft skills at the same time, presenting a basic element of design which will exploit the qualities of each new medium. A discussion of negative space is combined with a description of wire craft in sculpture, the creation of surface qualities with direct plaster techniques, articulation (joining together) of basic shapes with papier mache, and dimensional values with clay figures and constructions.

You need not follow this book from cover to cover. If you are interested in learning how to work with wood and carpenter's tools, begin with the wood projects in the chapters on easy carving and construction; or if you are interested in a pliable medium, turn to the chapter on clay (photo on facing page shows a project being done in classical style).

An important factor in the choice of a medium is the possession of tools. If you own basic metal working tools, such as soldering irons and tinsnips, try your hand first at a wire sculpture or a mobile. However, if you have no tools and don't wish to buy any, turn to the chapter on direct plaster.

Finally, if you just wish to test your sculptural aptitude before investing in materials and tools, try beginning with papier mache. This medium is one of the most exciting of the sculptural media presented in this book.

Even the greatest artists in any field learn their skills initially by copying the styles of other artists. Therefore, if you copy these projects exactly, you are preparing yourself to create your own, individual kind of sculpture.

CONTROLLING SPACE WITH WIRE SCULPTURE

Have you ever seen a statue in a room too small or with a ceiling too low? Perhaps the limbs seemed awkward and the shape less natural than if it had been standing in the space for which it was designed. Every sculpture is two things: a shape, and a volume of space affected by the shape. Not only should the limbs of a sculpture form harmonious relationships, but the whole figure should have an air of harmony with the space it displaces, surrounds, and occupies. The all-important emptiness through and around a sculpture is called "negative space."

Marble sculptures displace space as a bather displaces water. A wire sculpture (such as the dog in this chapter) displaces no space. The shape is merely an illusion. There is really nothing but space, cut up by a few lines of wire. However, a wire sculpture must create a feeling of appropriate bulk, or it will remain only a scrawl in the air. Some of the emptiness must be surrounded by and incorporated into the wires, becoming negative space.

This chapter presents two kinds of wire sculptures: stabiles and mobiles. Stabiles are rigid, free-standing figures. Mobiles are constructions designed to move in balanced patterns; they are shape-changing and space-changing sculptures.

THE TOOLS ARE SIMPLE

The basic tools for all wire sculpture are simple: a wire cutter, pliers of different sizes, a soldering iron and solder, glue, and wire in various lengths and diameters. Vises, C-clamps, a drill, and a hammer come in handy for specific projects. A mobile that has fins of sheet metal will also require tin snips, a taper file, a round file, steel wool, chisels, punches, and a block for pounding.

Enormous mobiles have been built with welded joints, but the amateur sculptor does not always have the skill or the equipment required for such ambitious projects.

CHOOSE THE MATERIALS

Always review the project before selecting the wire for a mobile. Some projects will require soft or brittle wire, whereas others will require springy, elastic wire. It is important to choose wire of a diameter that is appropriate to the composition and strong enough to support itself.

You must also decide whether to use straight lengths of wire or coils. Straight lengths are easier to handle and can always be bent into any curve. Coiled wire is very difficult to straighten, but is more common and serves perfectly well for most mobiles.

Aluminum wire in straight lengths is excellent for both stabiles and mobiles. It bends easily and forms rigid corners. However, it is too brittle to be straightened and reshaped and cannot be easily bent into tight curves. Copper or galvanized types are appropriate for almost any kind of sculpture, or regular clothes hangers can be used.

Most wire can be purchased at a hardware store or an electrical supply store. The mobiles described in this chapter make use of zinc alloy sheet and stiffened cloth. You may wish to experiment with still other materials, such as bits of wood veneer, paper, or plastic.

MEDIEVAL SWORDSMAN, 22 inches high, demonstrates importance of negative space and spatial unity for sculptural composition. Directions are on page 8.

STABILES—SCULPTURE THAT DOESN'T MOVE

In a successful stabile wire sculpture, all sides and dimensions of a figure can be viewed simultaneously. This transparency creates many interesting effects. The following three concepts should be kept in mind while trying your hand at constructing stabiles:

1. To create an illusion of surface, you must deal not only with the wires that form the outline of the surface, but also with the wires outlining surfaces behind and around it. No single area of a wire figure may be separated and finished independently.

2. On the other hand, since all sides of the figure are seen at once, a sculpture can be remarkably unified. An old art-school test of the merit of a figure is to pour a glass of water over it. The water is supposed to wet the whole figure, because all surfaces are supposed to be unified and flow into each other. The trick seldom works, especially on wire sculptures, but the idea is valid. Surfaces must relate to each other, or "work together" as the sculptor says. Each illusory surface must be stark and clear, but must flow into the same general movement, or else recede behind each other in a simple composition. You need not walk around such a figure to appreciate its harmony.

3. A stabile wire sculpture permits the continuation of lines and surfaces within the figure. For example, the wires that define the shoulders of the Medieval Swordsman, described on these two pages, continue their movement inside the figure. Lines are not terminated, but flow into the negative space of the figure, helping to create that negative space. Artistically, this effect tends to unify a figure. Emotionally, it suggests serenity and continuity with the surrounding space.

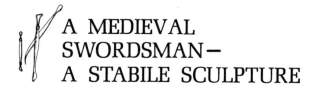

A MEDIEVAL SWORDSMAN— A STABILE SCULPTURE

This project can be built in one day's working time. Imitating its form, not copying it, should increase your grasp of the techniques of wire sculpture.

MATERIALS NEEDED

A block of wood two by eight, eight feet long

Two 36-inch lengths of aluminum wire (slightly heavier than coat hanger wire)

Six 36-inch lengths of aluminum wire (thinner gauge)

Epoxy resin

Heatless solder

Blue and yellow plastic film

PRIMARY WIRES create structure and dimensional movement, as well as representing features. Detail wires break up space to create planes.

CREATING THE FORM

Before you begin working with the wires, cut an 8-inch-square block of wood. Sand the wood to remove all rough edges.

Begin forming the figure by bending one 36-inch wire of the heavier gauge so that it outlines one side of the skirted figure (see drawing). Using a small drill or nail, make a hole in the wooden block and insert one end of the wire. (Make holes for securing the wires only as you need them — do not make them in advance.) Insert one end of the second heavy wire in the base and bend the length so that it outlines the figure from another angle. These two wires must define both the folds of the robe and the posture of the swordsman. Aluminum wire bends easily if you hold the two ends of the wire and bend the curve all at once.

Now bend the upper part of the second wire to suggest shoulders and a breastbone. Continue the line of the shoulders down inside the figure. The two wires should cross and blend together in a graceful form, touching only at the breastbone. At this meeting point, tie the wires in place with a little thread. Continue to work one wire at a time. The configurations of one wire will naturally suggest what to do with the next.

Bend one whole 36-inch wire of the thinner gauge to form another part of the skirt and insert in the base, well behind the shoulders. The upper part of this line should have the aspect of a spine. Tie it to the shoulder wire opposite the "V" of the breastbone. Bend the rest of the wire into an irregular loop to outline a head and neck in profile. At this point of construction, all wires should follow the same narrowing curve from the base forward toward the figure's right.

Insert a second 36-inch wire (thinner gauge) about midway between the two ends of the first heavier wire. Bend part of this wire into the nose shape as shown in the drawing, and the rest so that it suggests both a flap in the skirt and a knee. The curve of this wire, beginning at the knee and ending behind the left shoulder, will be opposite the curve made by all the previous wires together. It must be angled so that it parallels the simple curve of the left front wire as seen from the front.

This line is a device of composition which does many things for the figure. It builds up the left shoulder and creates a feeling of motion. It separates the space around the wires into inner and outer, thereby beginning an illusion of surfaces. The movement and direction of one wire are carried back into the other, creating a horizontal curve between wires to match the vertical curve along the wires. All imaginary surfaces between the wires will seem to wrap around the fold into the figure below its breastbone.

Bend the remaining length of this important wire sharply over the shoulder and form the left arm. This arm can be highly abstract. Curve the forearm to emphasize the roundness of the figure and rest the hand lightly on the hip.

For the sword arm, attach another 36-inch wire (thinner gauge) to the base of the neck, tie it in place at the shoulder, and bend it for the upper arm. Five inches below the shoulder, form the elbow, and five inches below the elbow, bend the wire once more to suggest a hand and a sword hilt. Use the remaining length of wire to form the sword. This may be shortened for balance.

When the figure is thus far completed, pull the tips of the wires out of the base, dab them with epoxy resin, and reinsert them.

ADDING DETAILS TO THE FORM

Connect a 21-inch length of thinner wire to the base of the neck and bend it intricately, forming a horizontal loop around the head and suggesting several details of the face, including eyes and chin.

Use the remaining wires, cut into various lengths, to form intricate patterns on the skirt. The purpose of these wires is to increase the illusion of surfaces by cutting up space into smaller units, to give the figure depth by separating the planes, and to add visual interest. Be careful not to overload the figure with such detail wires or it will become foot-heavy. Finish the details of the figure by tying the zigzags and spirals wherever they conveniently brush a supporting wire.

THE FINISHING TOUCHES

Once you have secured all the joints with thread, and the figure is formed to your satisfaction, mask the wooden base with newspapers and carefully coat all the tied joints with liquid aluminum glue or heatless solder. Then spray all the wires with flat black paint.

At this point, the figure might be considered finished. But the addition of a few bits of blue and yellow plastic film will improve the composition and add a medieval, stained-glass flair to the sculpture. The plastic film must be thin and transparent, so that no wires are hidden. Ordinary white glue, used sparingly, will hold the plastic to the painted wire and will dry clear. Use the plastic film to emphasize the illusions of surfaces. Where the blue and yellow film overlap, you will see a green that shifts as you move.

A DOG—A STABILE SCULPTURE

This project can be highly abstract in its creation. It is simpler in composition than the Medieval Swordsman, but basic construction steps are the same.

MATERIALS NEEDED

A block of wood two by eight, eight feet long

Five 36-inch lengths of straight wire of coat hanger gauge

Five 36-inch lengths of straight wire of thinner gauge

Epoxy resin

Heatless solder

Varnish or stain

CREATING THE FORM

Begin this project by cutting and sanding an 8-inch square block of wood.

Use the full lengths of each of the five heavier wires to form the general outline of the figure. Try to make a pleasing abstract form before actually suggesting a dog. One at a time, set the

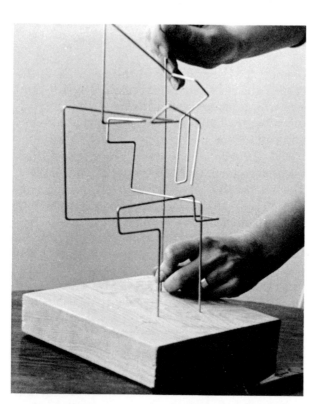

INSERT TIPS of the wires into wooden base one at a time and bend the wires into stark, unusual shapes, composed to lead from one to another.

BIND WITH TAPE any joints where the composed wires happen to touch. When sculpture is finished, replace tape with string, and coat with solder.

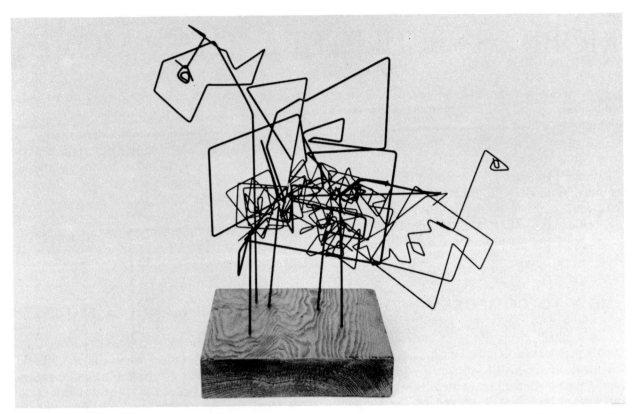

WHIMSICAL DOG, 12 inches high, upon completion, has five legs, and one eye dangling in the middle of his head. Clusters of wire, bent in triangles and squares create a feeling of mass in the lower center of the figure. The figure can be created in a few hours, and the materials cost less than one dollar.

wires in place and manipulate them, following these basic directions:

Make a hole in the base and insert one end of a heavier wire. At a point about eight inches up the wire, form a large, angular head. Add the remaining heavier wires to form shoulders, back, and haunches, bending them in straight lines and at angles only. Take care that each wire does not form a single limb or quarter, but intertwine them with the total unity of the sculpture in mind.

When the form is complete, lift the wire tips from the base, dab them with epoxy resin, and reinsert. Tie the wires where they happen to brush, and coat the joints with heatless solder.

When you have finished forming the abstract outline you want, begin to work out whimsical details to represent the animal. Take two wires, which should be thinner than the main wires, and form the tail and the eye, cutting off and discarding any extra length. Bend the last three wires into odd clumps of twisted triangles and squares, in keeping with the same shapes and angles you made in forming the general outline of the dog. Place these clusters within the figure, moving them around until the right arrangement appears. You are working now to create deliberate accidents. Use tape to hold an arrangement temporarily, and remember to view the arrangement from all sides.

Place all of the wire clusters in the lower center of the figure to deliberately create a feeling of weight. Your eye should be drawn to this part of the composition, which becomes the center of interest.

THE FINISHING TOUCHES

When all details seem right to you, tie the wires where they happen to brush, and coat the joints with heatless solder. Then mask the base with newspapers and spray all the wires with flat black paint. Remove the newspapers and coat the base with oil or varnish, or stain it.

MOBILES—SCULPTURE THAT MOVES

A good mobile is a stately kaleidoscope of forms and spaces opening and closing. Hanging mobiles are excellent home decorations, dividing the air space of a room and making lively the usual blankness of a ceiling or wall.

Although the mobiles presented in this chapter may be made with relatively simple materials and without mathematical engineering, they reflect the influence of Alexander Calder, whose museum-sized mobiles made the form popular.

HOW TO COMPOSE A MOBILE

A mobile must have a center of interest or some equally good device of composition. For example, the large metal mobile pictured on page 13 is merely a collection of small mobiles which move independently, but it is unified by the six fins hanging in its core. The fins become the center of interest and give a feeling of bulk and weight to the structure.

In a vertically composed mobile, the interest results from the variety and delicacy of parts. Notice that in the mobile pictured here the three

separate crossbars hanging directly below each other emphasize its vertical character.

In a mobile that extends horizontally all branches lead back to a single fulcrum. Therefore, the parts must be more unified, since no piece can move without affecting the balance of all other pieces. Note that the cloth mobile, shown on page 14, extends horizontally. No part can move without affecting the balance of the structure. It is an organic form with four balanced limbs.

HOW TO BALANCE A MOBILE

The arms of any mobile are nothing more than levers. Any lever balances when the weight and fulcrum-distance of one arm multiplied together equal the weight times the length of the other arm. The weight and fulcrum-distance are inversely proportional. For example, an adult can occupy a teeter-totter with a child if the child sits far out at one end while the adult sits up close to the fulcrum. Look closely at some of the mobiles pictured in this chapter for examples of small weights balancing larger weights. The

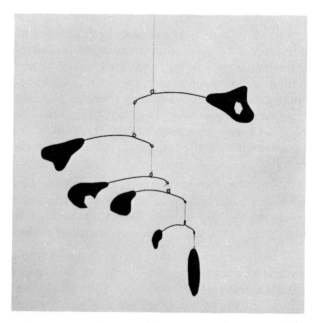

EACH FIN of this mobile balances the weight of all fins above it creating an elegant curve. To balance the series, begin at the bottom and work up.

DETAIL OF vertical mobile on facing page consists of five levers and six fins in series. Vary the shapes of the fins with cutouts and perforations.

smaller weights are always farther from the fulcrum than are the larger weights.

A mobile *could* be constructed mathematically from plans and equations or by working with scales and tape rules. However, in practice, all mobiles are constructed by sight. Slight imbalances often occur because of this procedure but also create interesting effects.

Here are two reminders that will help you in balancing a complicated series of parts by eye: If a fin, a group of fins, or any other weight hangs from a joint in a lever, all the weight will be exerted at the joint. If weight is distributed along a rigid bar (as happens when a fin is soldered to the end of a wire), then the length of the weight must be considered because the weight concentrates on an unpredictable center of gravity.

This art of balancing may sound complicated, but it really isn't difficult to master. If you are constructing a series of bars and fins, simply start with the lowest fin and work up one bar at a time. Check the total balance as you work.

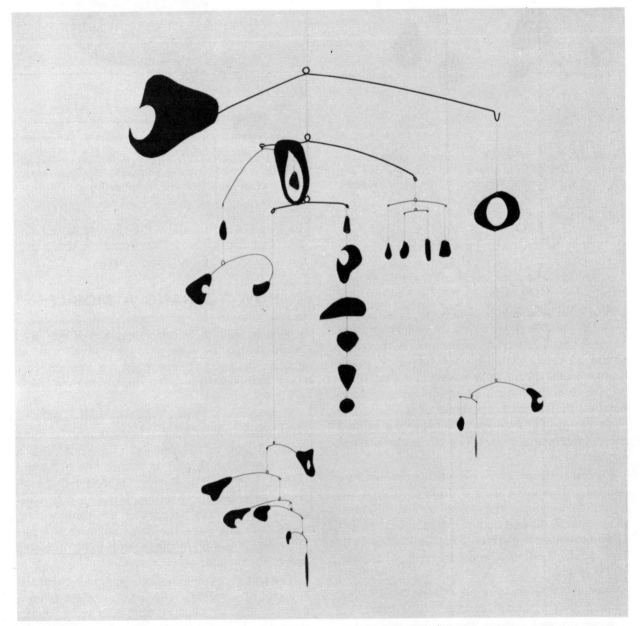

VERTICALLY COMPOSED mobile is easy to balance because arms and sections are independent. To create such a mobile, begin with the largest sections and create smaller details in harmony. Use various shapes and sizes, but unify the sculpture by repeating the patterns of balance on different levels.

HORIZONTAL MOBILE is created with a few densely related pieces which lead, visually and mechanically, to central fulcrum, by which it is hung.

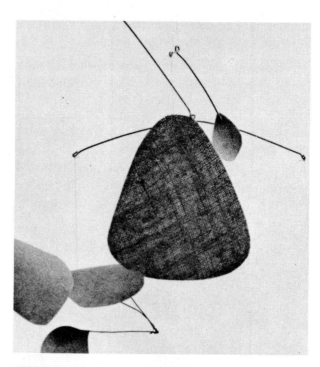

TEXTURED CLOTH, stiffened for use in mobile making, is both attractive and aesthetically valuable; cloth fins suggest both mass and delicacy.

MOBILES WITH SPECIAL TEXTURES

Texture and color make cloth an excellent substitute for sheet metal in mobile making, but cloth requires careful preparation.

Gather materials by buying or collecting some quarter yards of burlap, medium-weight cotton, or similar heavy cloth. Choose interesting, rough textures and plain, bold colors. Two or three related colors will form a more interesting composition than a whole spectrum of patches. The cloth mobile pictured on this page has related colors of blue and green. The wires and strings are also blue.

Before cutting any pieces, stiffen the cloth by painting it heavily with ordinary white glue, liquid plastic, or acrylic emulsion. You will need to apply several coats, allowing each coat to dry at room temperature. Never dry the coated cloth over heat. Heat and moisture will wilt glue-stiffened cloth.

Fasten cloth fins to wires or rods with epoxy resin, following the directions on the tube.

A word about design: The composition of the cloth mobile shown above is gayer and less intricate than that of most metal mobiles. Notice that the large oval fins allow the cloth texture to be seen and break up the surrounding space into more irregular, more intense areas.

HOW TO HANG A MOBILE

A mobile should be hung just above eye level where it may be seen against a blank wall or against drapery. There must be enough free space in this setting for the mobile to turn freely in all directions.

Mobiles can be hung from the ceiling using a small screw eye or hook. They can also be hung from an arm or bracket extending out from a wall. Use nylon thread or fishing line to hang a mobile, but don't use wire, since it will break from the constant twisting. If you use threads and want them to be part of the composition, make sure they are the same color as the fins and bars. If you want the threads to be invisible, use white thread.

The last step for hanging a mobile is to attach one end of a swivel (this can be taken from a fishing plug or leader) to the bottom of the thread or line and the other end to the fulcrum of your structure. A swivel will allow the mobile to spin easily in a slight draft.

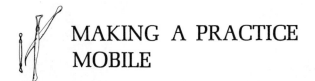

MAKING A PRACTICE MOBILE

The decorative mobile presented here provides an exercise for improving your techniques of construction. A diagram of all parts is shown on page 16. Each part has been given a letter for ease in following directions.

MATERIALS AND TOOLS NEEDED

Several square feet of 16-gauge zinc sheet

The long, bottom section of a coat hanger

A coil of 18-gauge galvanized wire

String

Needle-nose pliers

Tracing paper

Metal chisel

Hammer

Tin snips

File

Soldering iron

Metal punch

HOW TO PREPARE THE MATERIALS

Begin construction of this mobile by placing tracing paper over the diagram on page 16 and tracing the outline of the fins and the holes to be punched. Cut out the tracings and, using a pencil, outline each one on the zinc sheet, being sure to mark the holes. Cut out the metal pieces with tin snips and file their edges smooth. With a pencil, letter each piece as shown on the diagram.

Cut out the hole in piece B by laying the piece on a block of wood, then placing the beveled edge of a chisel on the tracing of the hole and hammering evenly. The chisel will cut like an old-fashioned can opener. With a punch, make holes for the strings in all pieces, as indicated.

Using the punch and needle-nose pliers, bend the piece of coat hanger to match wire 1 in the diagram. Cut two lengths of galvanized wire and bend them to match wires 2 and 3.

Assembling the Large Arm. Solder piece A in place on the straight end of wire 1, cut-out side down. Then tie pieces C, D, and E in place on piece B, letting piece D hang slightly lower than pieces C and E. (Don't be too concerned with the exact spacing of these pieces. You probably will want to restring the mobile by eye after painting it.) Now hang piece B from the hooked end of wire 1. This completes one arm of the

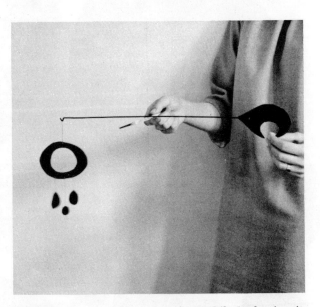

CLENCH THE TIP of a wire in a needle-nosed pliers, and with the other hand, bend the wire around the pliers to create either a hook or a loop.

BALANCE a complete arm of a mobile by letting it rest on the edge of a triangular file; at this point bend a loop to create a fulcrum.

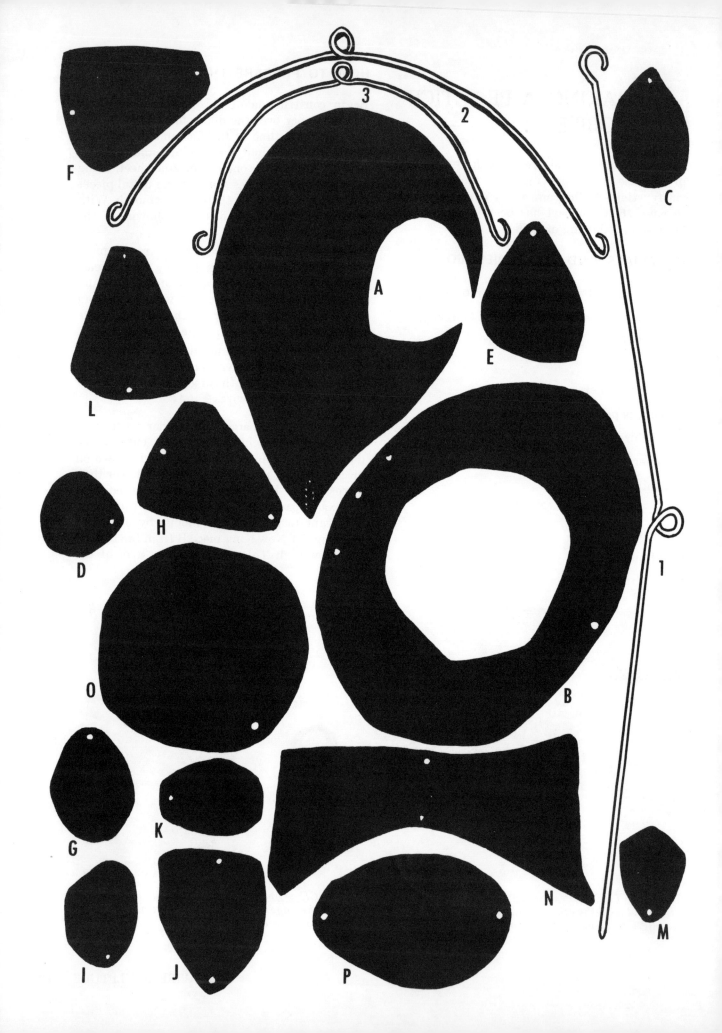

mobile. Be sure to check the balance. If either side of the arm hangs too low, correct it by rebending the fulcrum loop and shifting the loop toward the heavy side.

Assembling the Small Arms. Assemble pieces F, G, H, and I and hang them from wire 2, as shown in the photograph of the finished mobile. Correct the balance. Using a short string, connect the fulcrum loop of this arm to the fulcrum of the first arm.

Assemble pieces J, K, L, M and hang them from wire 3, as shown in the photograph. Correct the balance and hang the third arm below the second. The fins of these two arms should hang on a level. Hang pieces N and O on the end of a string and attach to the fulcrum of wire 3.

FINISHING AND PAINTING

Use piece P for the cap of the mobile and suspend wire 1 from its fulcrum. When all pieces are in place and balance to your satisfaction, the mobile is ready to be painted. This mobile may be painted any color, but we suggest that you use a flat black paint or some other flat spray paint. A flat color will enhance the composition as well as cover any nicks and dents in the fins.

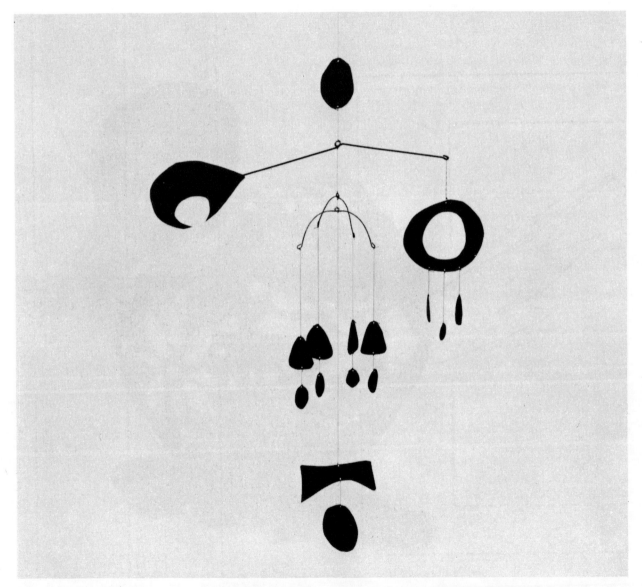

ALL THE PIECES for this completed sheet metal mobile are included in the life-size diagram on the facing page; instructions begin on page 15. Designed *to be hung in a small area or the corner of a room where it will turn in the slightest breeze, the mobile can be assembled and painted in two hours.*

SPECIAL SURFACES AND TEXTURES

Direct plaster sculpture is paradoxical. Although no tools or studied techniques are required, professional sculptors consider it extremely difficult. It allows for both modeling and carving, but these techniques are more appropriate to other materials. The speed with which direct plaster hardens or sets up can be a handicap. In a matter of minutes it can change from a creamy liquid to a grainy paste and then finally to an unworkable solid.

The potential of achieving special surface effects makes up for any difficulties that may be encountered when using direct plaster. The figure of a man in an overcoat, described at the end of this chapter, demonstrates what can be done with a plaster surface. Look at the coat. The plaster doesn't look at all like tweed or rayon, yet it suggests the folds and textures of a fabric. Such controlled and imitative effects are not possible with any other direct medium. Wire sculpture gives only the illusion of surface; papier mache yields an excellent surface, but one that is always the same. With either, there is little potential for imitation. Direct plaster not only yields interesting textures, but provides a potential for subtle, suggestive effects.

THE PLASTER TO USE

All of the sculptures shown in this chapter were made with casting plaster. This finer type of

PLAYROOM BIRD with curlicue wings combines spatial elements of wire sculpture and textural qualities of direct plaster modeling. Directions on page 25.

plaster can be purchased at an art supply house or a hardware store. Coarser plasters and plaster of Paris can also be used but are less desirable.

HOW TO MIX THE PLASTER

Use a shallow, flexible-plastic dishpan for mixing quantities of plaster. Leftover plaster that sets up can be loosened by flexing the bowl from beneath.

For a good consistency, use three parts plaster to two parts water. To mix one batch of plaster, pour two-thirds of a cup of water into the pan, then slowly sift a cup of plaster into the water until a small conical island forms above the surface. The more evenly you sift plaster, the stronger will be the mix. Using your fingers, stir the water and powder gently until it is mixed thoroughly. Tap the bowl briskly and allow the mixture to stand for a minute (but not longer).

TEXTURE AND CONSISTENCY OF PLASTER

Never add water to plaster after it is mixed, since this may accelerate the hardening process. When the plaster becomes stiff or crumbly, it is referred to as having "set up." Although not fully dry, it is no longer workable.

After mixing a batch of plaster, you will have about 10 minutes in which to apply it to a basic form before it sets up. During this time its consistency will change. If applied while still creamy, the plaster will dry to a smooth, strong texture. If it is applied after it has begun to stiffen, it will yield a grainy, pebbly texture. Many interesting surface effects can be created by merely juxtaposing these two textures.

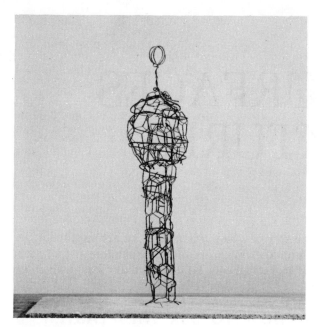

CHICKEN WIRE ARMATURE establishes the contours of a figure; pieces of wire should be bound tightly together to support the sculpture sturdily.

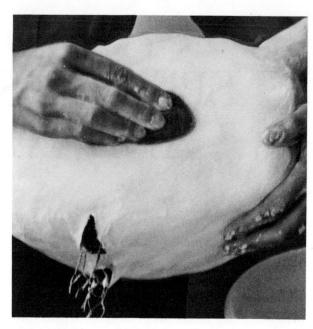

SCRAPING PLASTER with steel wool or with a rasp creates a unique, shiny surface which contrasts sharply with pebbly texture of unpolished plaster.

SUPPORTING MATERIALS AND ARMATURES

Direct plaster is almost always sculpted over a basic mount. This mount, called an armature, establishes the form of the sculpture. An armature used in a bas-relief usually consists of a wire screen attached to a wooden frame and therefore remains stationary. An armature for a free-standing sculpture is a skeleton created with materials that can be bent into supple and complex forms.

Direct plaster is seldom applied directly to an armature. It is first applied to some supporting material which gives it strength and shape, and the supporting material is applied to an armature. Ordinary gauze and cloth were used for the supporting materials in the sculptures pictured in this chapter. You will find that gauze permits free and fluid modeling.

MODELING OR FORMING A FIGURE

To model any figure, you must begin by roughly shaping the whole form over an armature. Do not try to complete any feature until the whole form is established.

Each feature must be built up gradually with or without a supporting material. For example, the boots of the figure on page 24 were modeled over single wires with no supporting material. Seven fresh applications of plaster were needed to form this feature. Meanwhile, modeling was progressing evenly over the rest of the figure.

SURFACE SCRAPING CAN BE USEFUL

The surface of a figure sculpted with direct plaster should be rough and spontaneous. Scraping and chipping can smooth direct plaster to a stony finish, but the resulting surface is usually dead and flat. Nevertheless, scraping can vary a surface that is too even or too grainy. Use a palette knife or a rasp (don't buy a special tool), to scrape a lifeless area until its texture pleases you. Scraping is also useful for correcting an unsatisfactory surface. Do not hesitate to destroy an area of a sculpture that displeases you. Scrape it away and start again.

If you want to create a sculpture that has a marble-like surface, don't work with direct plaster at all. Turn your energies to modeling in clay and casting in plaster or metal. It is always best to be true to the nature of your medium in creating a sculpture.

BAS-RELIEFS ARE LIKE PICTURES

A bas-relief is a sculpted form which has areas that project but do not stand entirely free from the background. The two landscape projects presented here and on the next two pages describe how direct plaster can be used in sculpting bas reliefs.

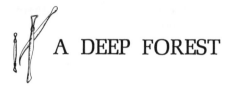 A DEEP FOREST

This bas-relief can be created with plaster soaked strips of cloth. It is very subtle in design, and the folds of cloth suggest shapes and forms.

MATERIALS NEEDED

Five pounds of plaster

Wooden frame

Sheet of wire screen

Large piece of cloth

Paint

Two eyelet screw hooks

Wire for hanging

MODEL, DESIGN AT THE SAME TIME

The wooden frame may be built or it may be purchased from an art supply store. Whether you decide to build or buy the frame, it should be of a size appropriate for hanging.

Screw two eyelet hooks into the back of the frame for eventual hanging, before you begin to work with the plaster. This avoids the possible jarring loose of finished plaster when the project is finished.

When the hooks are in place, cover the front of the wooden frame with a sheet of wire screen. Secure the screen with nails and trim the edges using a pair of tin snips. Cover the screen completely with patches of cloth or gauze dipped in plaster. Allow this ground to dry. Using a pencil, sketch a basic design of the relief on the plaster ground.

Cut up your cloth (an old sheet will do) in shapes and sizes as you need them, while the work progresses. Mix a cup of plaster to a creamy consistency. Dredge each piece of cloth, one at a time, in the plaster and quickly model it, allowing the folds of cloth to suggest billowing foliage. The large clumps of trees should stand much higher in relief than the smaller

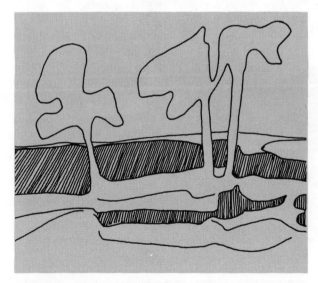

COMPOSITIONAL SKETCH of deep forest relief reveals vertical shapes of the trees, breaking the horizontal lines of foreground, background, and sky.

DREDGE EACH SQUARE of cloth in plaster and apply to sculptured surface; crumple plaster-soaked squares together to create highly raised modeling.

clump of trees, and should be closer to the center of the relief. Using thin strips of cloth, model horizontal shapes in the foreground and behind both clumps of trees to suggest depth and to unify the composition of the trees.

ADDING THE FINISHING TOUCHES

When the relief has had time to set up thoroughly, it can then be painted. First, spray the entire surface with flat, light olive paint. This will emphasize the textures and the modeling by cutting down reflections. Next, brush a thin black wash over the sky surface and a thicker black wash over the middle ground. (Directions for using washes are presented in the chapter on finishing a sculpture.) Over a very thin black wash on the foreground, lightly brush a yellow ochre wash so that the color will settle in the depressions. This color will bring the area of the sculpture closer to the viewer. To emphasize the contrasting textures of the trees, ground, and sky, outline the trees with a thick, black wash.

Using a white wash and a carefully wiped brush, paint the surface of the trees and their roots to create artificial highlights.

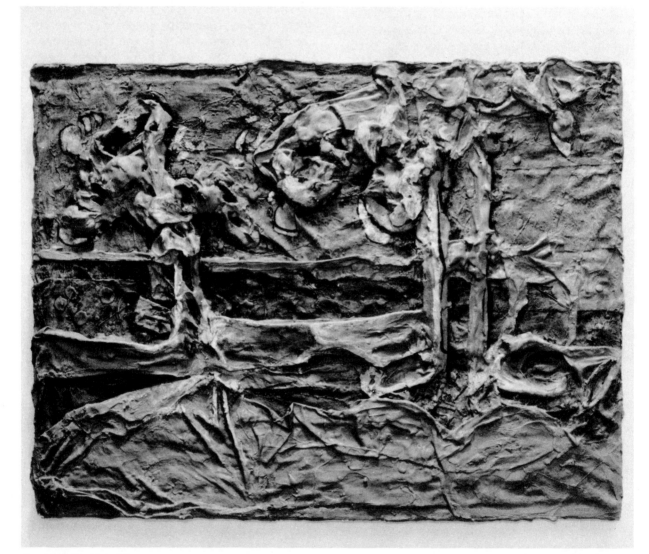

PLASTER RELIEF of a landscape with trees is built over a frame of chicken wire and wood; billowing foliage is suggested by the natural folds of cloth and plaster applied while fresh and creamy. The grainy texture of the sky results from applying plaster which has begun to stiffen. Directions on page 21.

A ROW OF TREES, with their shadows modeled in relief with direct plaster, create a lively pattern against a sunset sky which may be colored with blue, green, and yellow turpentine washes. The scrolls on the second tree from the left are formed with thin cloth strips that have been dredged in plaster.

A STYLIZED FOLK PICTURE

The relief shown above — a row of trees — is a stylized folk picture. It does not attempt to project a sense of perspective and realism.

MATERIALS NEEDED

Five pounds of plaster

Wooden frame

Sheet of screen, hardware cloth, or chicken wire

Two eyelet screw hooks

Wire for hanging the relief

Roll of gauze or an old sheet

Paint

BUILDING THE GROUND OR SURFACE

For this project, you can either build a wooden frame or buy one at an art supply store. The size of the frame should be suitable for hanging in your home. Screw two eyelet hooks into the back of the frame for eventual use in hanging.

Stretch a sheet of wire screen, hardware cloth, or chicken wire over the front of the frame, nailing it in place. Trim the edges with a pair of tin snips. Then cut a roll of gauze or old sheet into several dozen 4-inch squares.

Mix a full cup of plaster to a creamy consistency. To form a flat surface or ground, dredge each square of cloth, one at a time, in the plaster and place on the wire-covered frame, making sure each piece slightly overlaps the other.

Mix a second batch of plaster and let it stand until it loses its creaminess. Spread this mixture over the whole ground until the surface is flat and the screen texture is completely hidden.

BUILDING UP THE RAISED AREAS

Cut forty or fifty 1-inch squares of cloth. These will be used to form the trees. Make a third batch of plaster. One at a time, dredge each square in the plaster until each is heavily coated. Crumple each square and press it onto the ground area. Work quickly with each piece of cloth until you have built up the main features of your relief to the height you desire.

Apply fresh plaster with your fingers to fill in and smooth the raised surface.

The relief should now have two levels: the background of sky and the raised modeling of the row of trees and the foreground. Embellishments can be made on the trees and background by using thin strips of gauze or cloth that have been soaked in plaster, or by modeling plaster directly when it begins to set up. In the relief pictured here, cloth was used to form the swirls on one of the trees and the shadow patterns across the foreground.

When the plaster used in forming details of trees and foreground has set up, the panel is ready for the finishing touches. Apply a fresh coat of plaster directly to the wooden frame so that the entire panel looks like a solid piece of plaster, and let it dry thoroughly.

After the panel is thoroughly set up, you may wish to paint it. The entire relief shown on page 23 was coated with ivory gloss wall paint. Details of the trees and shadows were painted with yellow, blue, and red oil colors, which were slightly diluted with turpentine.

You may brush various colors of turpentine washes over numerous areas of the relief to create a color scheme. (For directions in the use of washes, see the chapter on surface effects of paints and patinas.)

FREE-STANDING SCULPTURES

A free-standing sculpture is a three-dimensional shape, a figure in the round. What we generally call statues fall into this class, but reliefs do not. Sometimes a sculptor composes several figures in a group, but usually sculptures in the round are limited to single, simple forms. While a relief can display a picture-like landscape, a free-standing sculpture is inevitably an animal or human form, or an abstract form related to human form.

Free-standing sculptures using direct plaster require three-dimensional armatures, unlike the flat frames used to mount reliefs. Each plaster figure requires its own special skeleton.

The use of window screen and chicken wire makes almost any armature simple to create. These materials can be easily bent into the most complex forms and yet are strong enough to support the weight of the plaster. Occasionally, you may need to add a heavier wire or rod inside the shape of the screen to support a plaster limb.

PLASTER MAN in a long, old-fashioned coat typifies the simplicity of subject basic to most free-standing sculptures. Instructions are on page 27.

A PLASTER BIRD WITH WIRE WINGS

This project is extremely simple in design and construction. The armature is made of chicken wire and is hollow except for the heavier wires used to support the solid feet. The finished project is suitable for displaying outdoors or as a decoration for a child's room.

MATERIALS NEEDED

Five pounds of plaster

Sheet of chicken wire (5 ft. x 1 ft.)

Thin copper wire or tape

Gauze or cloth

Two 20-inch lengths of heavy wire

Cloth

Several lengths of 18-gauge galvanized wire

Paint

SHAPING THE ARMATURE

Begin shaping the armature by cutting the sheet of chicken wire into a rectangular piece 12 x 25 inches. Using a piece of string, tie the narrow sides together forming a cylinder. With a pair of tin snips, make several slits in the two ends of the cylinder. Overlap the slit ends so that the cylinder becomes egg-shaped, and secure these ends with thin copper wire or tape. This balloon of wire will be the bird's body.

At the bottom of the body, attach two small stubby cylinders of chicken wire a few inches apart with copper wire or tape. These small cylinders will form the joints of the legs. To make the bird's neck, make a cylinder of chicken wire that is 4 inches long and 6 inches around. Tape the neck solidly to the body. Make the head by cutting a piece of chicken wire 5 x 12 inches and, in the same manner as you formed the body, shape this sheet of wire into a smaller egg. After you have taped the head to the neck, you may wish to tilt both forms to suggest a cockiness.

PLASTERING THE BODY

Cut fifty or more 3-inch squares of gauze, and mix a cup of creamy plaster. Dredge each square of gauze in the plaster, one at a time, and spread them over all of the armature except the legs, letting each piece overlap the other. When the armature is covered, mix two cups of plaster. Spread the fresh plaster over this covering with your fingers until the cloth texture is hidden. Apply plaster that is very creamy over the back of the figure so that the final surface displays a smooth texture. After it sets up, you may rub this area with steel wool to further enhance the texture. Using plaster that has begun to thicken, apply a final surface coat to the chest and head to achieve a coarse and pebbly texture.

FORMING THE FEET

Once the plaster over the main part of the armature has set up, begin forming the feet. Bend the two 20-inch lengths of heavy wire into identical shapes of webbed feet, making them big enough to balance the body. Tape the feet to the exposed leg stumps and cover these lower extremities with heavily plastered cloth. Make sure the figure balances. When the cloth is in place, apply fresh plaster to the feet until they are thick and strong. Apply a final coat of plaster that has begun to thicken to achieve a coarse surface.

FORMING THE BEAK

Bend the two 18-gauge wires into "V" shapes. Using a pointed tool, punch four holes in the bird's face at the appropriate position for an upper and lower beak. Insert the tips of one bent wire into the two top holes and the tips of the second bent wire into the two lower holes so that the points of the two "V's" are an inch or so apart. Cover with pieces of gauze that have been dredged in plaster and add enough plaster over the surface to achieve the appropriate size.

FORMING THE WINGS AND TAIL

Bend some 18-gauge wire into curlicues to form two wings and a double tail. Make them as fantastic as you please. Here is a chance for you to vary the basic design considerably. These appendages will not be covered with plaster. Punch holes in the body for attaching the ends of the wings and tail, and insert the tips of the wires in the holes, making sure that each tip is long enough to reach across to the opposite wall of the figure. Secure each wire with a dab of fresh plaster at the opening.

THE FINISHING TOUCHES

You can spray the entire finished form with light olive green paint. Use light blue oil paint to color the beak. A band around the neck and flower patterns on the body in the same color will make this figure lively indeed.

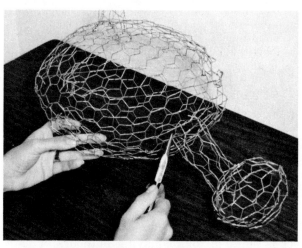

BUILD THE ARMATURE for this bird with simple oval shapes made from chicken wire; fasten shapes together by twisting bits of wire through the mesh.

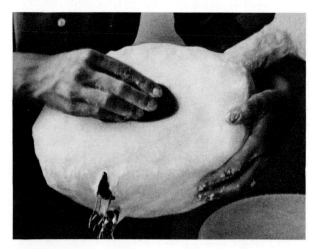

POLISH THE BACK and the head of the figure with steel wool to create a glossy texture that will contrast with the feathery and unpolished breast.

SHAPE EACH FOOT from a single heavy wire and attach it to the exposed stump of the leg; cover feet and legs with large squares of plaster-soaked cloth.

PIERCE A HOLE in the side of the bird using a sharp tool and insert the tip of a wire forming the wings or tail; secure the joint with plaster.

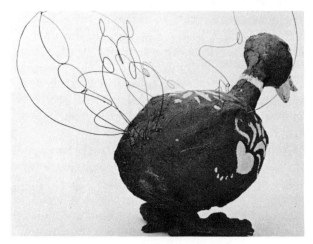

LARGE FEET provide a sturdy balance for the completed bird's plump body. Graceful wings and a fanciful double tail relieve the plainness of the form.

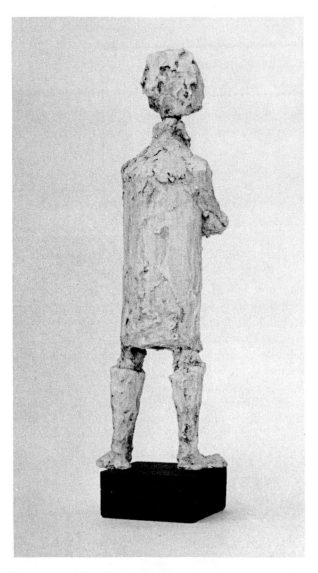

YOUNG GIRL with windblown hair is modeled in plaster, and is the companion in style and construction of plaster man pictured to the right and page 24.

ERECT FIGURE of plaster man, viewed from the back, is sculpted over armature of a few thin wires and a cylinder of screen, which is shown on page 29.

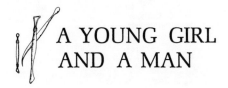

A YOUNG GIRL AND A MAN

These two figures were constructed in similar fashion, but their compositions and surface effects are very dissimilar.

The frail figure of the girl forms a soft, crescent-shaped curve which is repeated in the folds of the dress and the waves of her hair.

Therefore, the composition consists of only one long vertical line which is broken slightly by the neck and bust. The fluid textures of the plaster follow this vertical line like wax-drippings on a candlestick. This texture matches the flowing shape.

The figure of the man is a stark, angular composition, composed of several cylinders and globes. The shoulders, forearms, bottom of the coat, tops of the boots, and the feet form definite horizontal lines which cut across the stiff-looking torso. A surface which is grainy and jagged, especially around the turned-up collar, is in harmony with the composition.

MATERIALS NEEDED FOR GIRL

Two pounds of plaster, more or less

Square of window screen, 12 x 12 inches

Scrap of window screen, a few inches square

Two 36-inch aluminum wires, any gauge, or an equivalent length of some other stiff wire

Block of wood (two-by-four), 5 inches long

Nails

Tape or thin wire for tying

Paint

MAKING THE GIRL'S ARMATURE

The figure will be almost 20 inches in height, including the base. Cut a block of wood five inches long from a piece of two-by-four. Using a pair of tin snips, cut a piece of window screen roughly 1 foot square, and form it into a cone-shaped cylinder, securing it with string or thin wire. (The shape can be lopsided to suggest the girl's willowy posture.) Cut tabs in the bottom of the cone and nail the tabs to the wooden base. Insert an aluminum wire inside the cylin-

der, letting one end protrude at the top. To form the girl's head, twist a single loop on the end of the wire and cover it with a small piece of screen. Now mask the wooden base with newspaper, and keep it covered until the figure is finished.

MODELING AND FINISHING TOUCHES

Using plaster which has a creamy consistency, work very quickly and apply layer upon layer directly to the armature to build up the limbs, folds of the dress, and the head. Each feature of the figure should be kept at equal stages of completion while applying the plaster.

After the features have been formed to your satisfaction, allow the plaster to set up. Bend wires, from 2 to 5 inches long, to imitate hair lines. Use an awl or an ice pick to poke holes in the head for inserting these wires. Secure the wires in place and cover each lightly with creamy plaster.

Paint the figure with a white enamel. Over this coat of paint, brush a turpentine wash of green, allowing the color to settle in the folds of the dress. Unmask the base and finish it with oil, stain, or paint.

ROLL A CONE of window screen, supported by a single wire, and fasten it to a wooden base; add a bit of screen over which the girl's head will be modeled.

WILLOWY POSTURE of girl is emphasized by the loose flowing lines of her hair and gown and the casual positioning of her arms behind her back.

MATERIALS NEEDED FOR MAN

Two pounds of plaster, more or less

Rectangle of window screen, 16 x 12 inches

Scrap of window screen

Four 36-inch aluminum wires, to be cut into various lengths, or an equivalent quantity of some other stiff wire

Block of wood (two by four), 4 inches long

Nails

Tape or thin wire for tying joints

Paint

MAKING THE MAN'S ARMATURE

Cut a block of wood for the base. Using a pair of tin snips, cut a piece of screen 16 inches wide, bend it double, and roll it into a cylinder 8 inches high and 3 inches in diameter. Secure this shape with string or wire. Form the two legs by bending two 26-inch aluminum wires double. Form the two feet by bending thin loops in the doubled ends. Insert the straight ends of these wires into the fold of the cylinder and wire them in place. Nail the feet to the wooden base. Mask the base with newspaper, but without covering the feet.

At the shoulder height on one side of the body, insert a 13-inch wire completely through the body cylinder so that it protrudes on the other side. Bend the two ends of the wire to form arms crossed squarely over the chest. Twist another wire into a coil with one end extending several inches. Attach this wire to the top of the cylinder to form a head and neck, bending the coil forward to suggest a curve in the spine. Form the head by cutting a small piece of screen and taping it over the coil.

MODELING AND FINISHING TOUCHES

Using creamy and grainy plaster, quickly model the coat, legs, arms, shoulders, and head. You won't need much plaster to form the coat, but the other features will require many layers.

Paint the completed figure with a white enamel and brush with a thin wash of burnt umber. Uncover and finish the base with oil, stain, or paint.

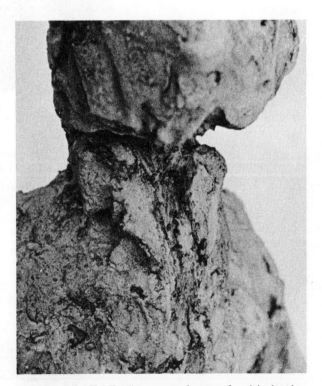

FIRST APPLICATION of plaster to the man's armature will barely cover the torso and head; final modeling will begin on coat with next batch of plaster.

MAN'S CRAVAT offers a good example of imitative plaster textures. The face is not modeled realistically, but is merely suggested by a swirling textural effect.

THE INTRIGUING MEDIUM OF PAPIER MÂCHÉ

The perceptiveness of children's art has been esteemed for many years. Children sometimes capture the essentials of a figure while drawing it freely and imaginatively. In doing so, they are abstracting by instinct. An adult can easily imitate childish art, but he is more of an artist if his own adult perceptions of form are developed.

Papier mache has built-in advantages for contending with the problem of form. A papier mache figure is constructed part by part rather than modeled. Thus, an uncertain beginner can wrestle with separate forms and not be concerned at first with forming a whole composite figure. He merely needs to articulate, or fit together, the completed parts properly. Since papier mache can be easily reworked, this joining of parts is not difficult.

The availability of durable polymer emulsion, has transformed papier mache into an intriguing adult medium. With the aid of this emulsion, figures can be sculpted that would not be duplicated in any traditional medium.

SUGGESTIONS FOR ESTABLISHING FORM

Sculptured figures are not always composed of simple cones, cubes, and primary shapes; but recognition of such forms in nature will help the sculptor to compose and unify his figures. For example, the body of a dog may be seen as

BOY ON STILTS is modeled in papier mache, using chicken wire, wood, clay, cloth, and string to create various details. Instructions are on page 40.

a cylinder, the neck as a cylinder, the skull as a globe, and the jaws as two trapazoidal boxes. Once recognized, these shapes can be built into the armature of a figure and thus serve as a basis for articulating the parts. This was done for the barking dog shown on page 36. The articulation of basic forms was as important to the composition of this sculpture as is the bow-shaped curve of the figure from muzzle to tail.

Always try to control the number and kind of shapes in any sculpted figure. Remember that a sculpture is not primarily a three-dimensional photograph of some object, but an object itself. It contains certain basic forms which have been harmonized into a single form. Look carefully for perceptions of form in the figures of the boy, bird, fish, reptile, and dog shown in this chapter.

ARMATURES FOR CONTOUR AND POSTURE

An armature for a papier mache sculpture must determine the contours as well as the posture of the figure. In fact, the armature is the figure and the papier mache is merely a skin.

Any material that supports itself can be used for an armature. (For example, carved pieces of styrofoam can produce very interesting figures.) The projects in this chapter are built over armatures of wire, screen, and foil.

An armature may be extremely simple, or involve several stages of construction. The finished bust, shown on the next page, was built over an armature of chicken wire combining three shapes taped together: an ovoid, a cylinder, and a flattened half-ovoid for the shoulders. These shapes were roughly covered with papier mache. Then the muscles of the neck, jaw, forehead, and nose were shaped in chicken wire and window screen and taped over the rough covering of papier mache. These features were immediately finished with papier mache. The eyes and lips were too delicate to be shaped with wire or screen. Instead, they were modeled in waterbase clay, patched right onto the papier mache, and covered immediately with more papier mache. In a sense, this clay was part of the armature. The ears were built separately over tiny armatures of wire and foil, constructed like a kite. They were finished with papier mache before being attached to the head.

START WITH PAPER STRIPS

Cut newspapers into strips, triangles, ovals, crescents, and yokes of various sizes and shapes. For interesting variations, when you don't intend to paint the finished figure, use all colored comics, or all want ads.

Some recipes for papier mache call for soaking the paper in a kind of gruel, which is easily applied, but which leaves a sodden unflexible surface. The projects shown in this chapter were created with dry scraps of newspaper dipped in a binder and spread carefully over the armature in overlapping patterns. To make application easier, some of the armatures were first wrapped with aluminum foil.

GLUES YOU CAN USE

Glues, wallpaper paste, and many other binders can be used for applying papier mache; however, flour and water paste and polymer emulsion are considered the most effective. These two binders and their surface possibilities are discussed below.

Make flour and water paste by mixing ¼ to ½ cup of white flour with a few spoonfuls of water. Stir the mixture until it becomes a smooth dough. Then add water until the dough becomes the consistency of cream. Only a limited surface-area of papier mache bound with this paste may be applied to a figure at each sitting. Allow the figure to dry in the sun or over low heat before continuing the application process.

Acrylic polymer emulsion is available at art supply stores. This binder has major advantages over all other binders. It is durable,

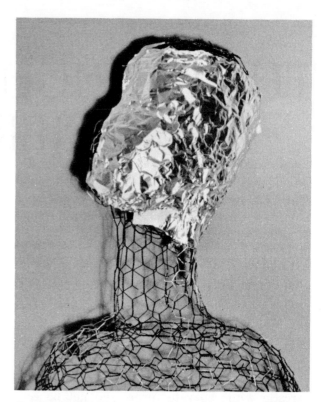

BASIC SHAPES, such as ovals and cylinders, can be created easily with chicken wire and fastened together with tape or wire to form complex armatures.

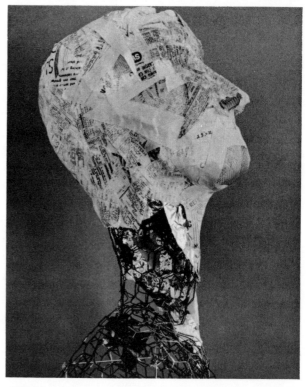

STAGES OF CONSTRUCTION shown in this armature are: basic shapes; aluminum foil skin; prime coating of paper strips and glue; wire screen details.

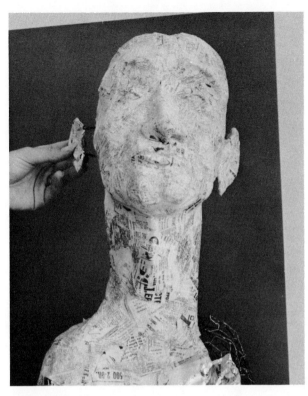

EXPOSED TIPS of armature wire within the ear are jabbed into the papier mache skin. Tape these features in place and cover joints with papier mache.

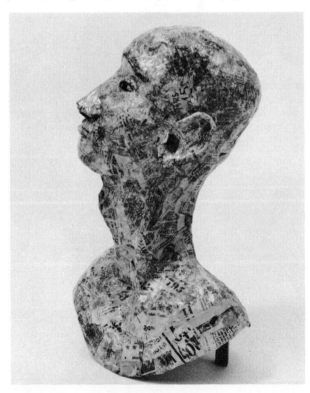

VARNISHED NEWSPRINT surface, raised eyebrows, and arrogant tilt of head make this sculpture more a matter of artistic satire than of beauty.

waterproof, and dries so rapidly that a figure can be constructed without pause. It is very cohesive, thus facilitating work on tricky details and guaranteeing a tighter surface. For greater elaboration of surface effects, combine other acrylic products and acrylic paints with polymer emulsion.

FINISH AND SURFACE POSSIBILITIES

Although lacking the imitative qualities of direct plaster, the surface rendered by papier mache is excellent in itself and should not be over-decorated. It possesses a sculptural value that more elaborate, traditional materials occasionally lack. Because of its peculiar texture, papier mache figures appear ponderable and touchable and seem to fill up the space they displace. A papier mache surface seems to carry your eye around corners to surfaces you can't really see without walking around the figure.

Flour and water surfaces may be varnished for durability and surface effect. The surface of the bust shown on this page was varnished and finished with a thin turpentine wash of black oil around the eyes and in the natural shadow areas. The exotic figure of a bird shown on page 35 was varnished and then sprayed with flat black paint.

Polymer surfaces do not need varnishing, although a brushed coat of emulsion helps to protect a figure.

To create a glossy surface, brush acrylic modeling paste heavily over the figure. Smooth this paste with a dripping wet brush. If this process is repeated several times, the papier mache texture can be entirely disguised.

Allowed to harden slightly, acrylic modeling paste acts like a sticky clay and can be used to create delicate features. Simply spread a lump of modeling paste on a polymer surface and allow it to set. Then model the feature. Tools will work better than fingers in this instance.

Decorations of twine can be laid on any papier mache surface. Soak the twine in polymer emulsion, then arrange it on the surface, temporarily taping it in place if necessary. Four of the sculptures shown in this chapter have twine decorations: the tortoise, the puppy, the pterodactyl, and the boy.

AN EXOTIC BIRD

Here is a project to be copied minutely if you are still vague about the craft of papier mache. Most of the projects that follow involve such basic materials as chicken wire, straight lengths of aluminum wire, masking tape, aluminum foil, strips of paper, and flour and water paste or polymer emulsion. The need for additional materials is noted in the projects themselves.

FORMING THE ARMATURE

Bend a 17-inch piece of soft, heavy wire into the shape of a long-necked bird in profile. One third of this length forms the neck and head, while the rest forms an oval body. The head is a tiny oval tilted downward, and the neck curves gracefully in a figure "S". Close the large oval by twisting the wire around itself at the base of the neck. Secure this joint with masking tape. To form the bird's ribcage, bend a second wire into another oval slightly smaller than the body. Tape it to the bird's backbone slightly nearer the neck than the tail, and again to the bottom of the body near the tail. The two ovals should be at right angles to each other.

Wrap a single sheet of aluminum foil around the body and fasten it with tape. Wrap and tape another sheet of foil around the neck so that it tapers toward the head and slightly overlaps the first sheet. At this overlap, form the shoulders by shaping the foil into a smooth curve. Roll some scraps of foil into a ball for the head and wedge it in place.

APPLYING PAPER TO THE BODY

Now cut a heap of newspaper scraps and make a paste of flour and water. Dredge the scraps one by one in the paste and, beginning at the base of the neck, smoothly spread them over the armature so that each piece overlaps the other. Make sure that each scrap is saturated with paste but not dripping. Cover the back first, then the breast, then the remaining parts of the body, allowing each section to dry and harden before working on the next.

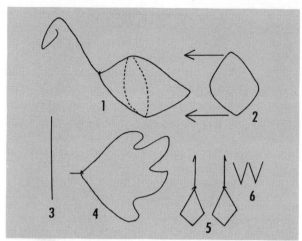

SIMPLE WIRE SHAPES create armature. Wires 1 and 2 form bird's body; wire 3 supports tail; wire 4 is a wing; wires 5 and 6 form feet and the beak.

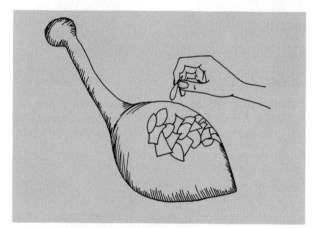

COVER BODY WIRES with aluminum foil; then cover the foil smoothly with scraps of paper soaked in flour and water paste, beginning with the back.

ATTACH LEGS by piercing wires into the papier mache skin; tape securely in place, wrap with aluminum foil for added bulk; cover with papier mache.

LEGS, FEET, TAIL, WINGS, AND BEAK

While the body covering is drying, bend two 7-inch wires to form the legs and feet. The webbed feet should be large for balance and grace. Cover the feet with foil. When the body covering is completely dry, bend the top ends of the leg wires into hooks and poke them into the appropriate places. Secure the legs with tape and check the bird's balance. (Weight should be concentrated in front of the legs so that the bird will lean forward.) Now mold the thighs with paper and paste. Cover the feet smoothly with tape so that they will be flexible enough to adjust the bird's balance when the wings and tail are added.

Cut a 6-inch piece of wire for the tail. Cover it with double strips of foil about an inch wide, leaving one tip of the wire bare. Cover the foil with papier mache and allow it to dry. Reinforce any sharp edges with masking tape. Jab the bare wire tip into the body shell at the appropriate place, securing it with tape. Cover the joint with papier mache.

Bend two 17-inch wires into identical, fanciful wire wings. Cover the wires with foil, leaving two prongs bare on each wing for fastening to the body. Mold the foil with your fingers into natural curves. Cover the wings with papier mache, one side at a time and allow them to dry. Cover any sharp edges with tape, and fasten the wings to the body at the proper angle. Secure the joints with tape and disguise them with papier mache.

Form an open beak with two short pieces of wire jabbed into the head and wrapped with foil. Cover the foil with papier mache. Make a topknot by attaching a small bead to each of three thin wires, and jabbing the wires deeply into the head.

THE FINISHING TOUCHES

Balance the bird carefully on its feet and stiffen the feet with papier mache, allowing them to dry thoroughly. Seal the figure with several coats of spar varnish.

CROWING BIRD has a skeleton of wire which determines the graceful composition of its neck, wings, and tail even before any papier mache is applied to its surface. Variations on this figure are possible in the shape of wings and tail and in surface decorations; follow the basic directions given above.

BARKING PUPPY has loaf-shaped body to which the head and limbs are attached one at a time. The head involves a separate armature of window screen which is covered with papier mache before it is connected to the body; ears and tail are formed with heavy wires covered with foil and papier mache.

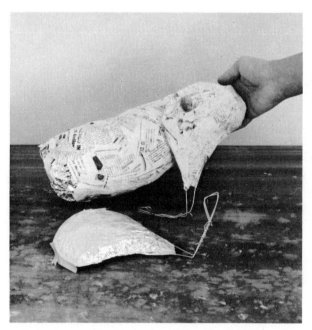

DOG'S HAUNCHES are shaped with wire and foil and taped in place on roughly formed body. Model the natural joints carefully with papier mache.

A PLAYFUL PUPPY

Do not attempt to sculpt a complex figure like a dog without referring to a living model or else to clear photos or drawings. Your composition should be based on direct observation of nature. Construct the separate parts of your armature to match the relative sizes and shapes you see in your model. Several days were spent in constructing this lively figure over a complex armature of chicken wire, aluminum rods, and window screen.

An unusual detail of this sculpture is the collar, which was added after the figure was finished and painted. The collar was made from a strip of screen which was covered directly with polymer papier mache, decorated with string and secured around the puppy's neck.

A WHIMSICAL FISH

with additional pieces of wire, finished with papier mache, and then attached to the body.

The figure was smoothed with acrylic modeling paste and painted with acrylic blue. It may be mounted on a base or merely set out on a shelf for display.

The solid, boney planes of this fish's head dissolve through a simple, tapering curve into the slender, weightless tail to suggest a rapid forward motion.

The body shell of this fish was built around three coat hanger wires, forming a backbone and a rib cage. These wires were twisted together at the gills and the base of the tail. Two loops of wire, forming the jaws, and two wires bent double for the eyes, were secured to the twisted wires at the gills.

This armature was then wrapped in foil and the body shell was modeled with papier mache, leaving the twist of wires at the tail uncovered. The double tail was modeled over a wire frame and was twisted together with the bare skeletal wires. This joint was wrapped with tape and covered with papier mache. Pectoral fins, dorsal fin, and tongue were constructed independently

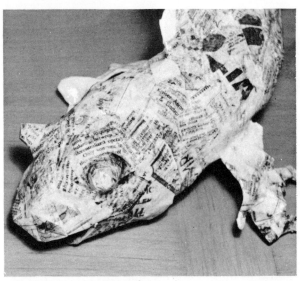

NEWSPAPER SCRAPS dipped in flour and water paste allow for the delicate modeling of this fish's gills and fins. A coathanger forms the skeleton.

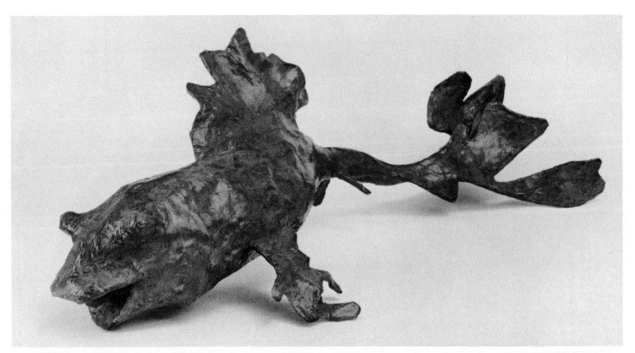

SWIMMING FISH has a naturally compact form, emphasized by the contrast of its lacy fins. Construct the head and body first as a single unit, modeling the fish's sides in two smooth and simple planes which end at the gills. Form the outline of each fin with a length of wire, cover with papier mache, and attach.

A FLYING REPTILE, THE PTERODACTYL

This flying monster has a wingspan of 54 inches, yet is light enough to hang by three strands of thread. Before you begin to construct such a massive figure, give some thought to making it look plausibly airborne. For example, you may want to tilt the body forward, lowering its beak as if the creature were scanning the earth.

Form the body and head with chicken wire and cover this armature with foil and polymer papier mache. Then pierce a 36-inch aluminum rod completely through the figure at the shoulders. Bend this rod on both sides of the figure to form the first joints of the wings. Add another 36-inch wire to each wing, overlapping about ten inches of the first wire to form a second joint. Wrap the overlapping lengths with masking tape. Then bend each wing into five more diminishing sections and joints.

From each wingtip, stretch a thin piece of copper wire to small wire tabs inserted in the rear corners of the body. Covered with papier mache, these tabs become claws. Fold large sheets of foil over these wires to create the wings and cover both sides with 4-inch squares of polymer-soaked paper.

Form the tail and claws on both wings and feet with bits of wire and insert in the appropriate places. Finish with papier mache. Model the eyes and nostrils with acrylic modeling paste. Decorate the under-surfaces of the wings with twine soaked in polymer. Brush a coat of gesso over the whole figure. Paint the figure "earth" colors, such as ochre and burnt siena.

UNFINISHED WINGS, enormous in proportion to the creature's body, reveal a kite-frame armature of wire and foil to be covered with papier mache.

AIRBORNE REPTILE hangs by nylon threads attached to his front claws and tail so that the wings support the body as they would in natural flight. In reality, pterodactyl's wings were formed by single, elongated toe bones supporting leathery membranes. Papier mache suggests a similar leathery surface.

A GROUND-HUGGING TORTOISE

A feeling of ground-hugging immobility has been created in this sculpture through the use of one basic shape—the hexagon. A line drawn between the limbs, head, and tail of this tortoise would form an irregular hexagon. The chicken wire used in the armature had a hexagonal mesh.

THE ARMATURE AND ITS COVERING

Begin construction of the tortoise by cutting two large ovals of chicken wire roughly the same size. Cut two broad tabs on opposite edges of one oval and fold the tabs up to form the side of the shell. Connect the two ovals so that the upper shell overhangs the tab sides and leaves the two ends open. Bend the ovals to the right shape and cover with foil. Then crudely cover the body shell with papier mache.

Form the legs by making four cylinders of chicken wire which are long enough to shove a few inches into the shell cavity. Bend the tubes for knees. Tape the legs in place at the corners of the shell openings and cover them with the usual skins of foil and papier mache.

Make a longer, tapering cylinder for the neck. Form a head with two round-sided triangles of window screen, one large and the other smaller. Attach this head to the narrow end of the neck and shove the other end into the body cavity between the front legs. Tape in place and wrap with foil. Cover the head and neck with papier mache, modeling the head and mouth carefully. Crease the skin of the neck to suggest folds of flesh. Model nostrils and eyes with acrylic paste, using a palette knife to shape the paste. Stretch foil over any openings in the shell, billowing the foil into the shell, and cover with papier mache.

Form the segments of the upper shell by cutting window screen into small hexagons and trapezoids. Starting at the center of the shell tape each segment to the shell until it is covered from edge to edge. Tape each segment so tightly that it bulges. Cover these wire segments with papier mache.

Paint the shell with white gesso, an acrylic substance. Clarify shell segments by outlining each segment with polymer soaked twine.

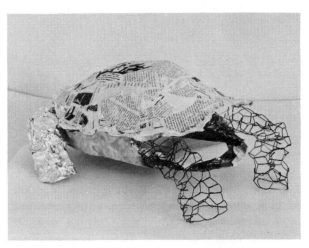

FORM SHELL with two sheets of chicken wire covered roughly with papier mache; form legs of chicken wire, secure inside shell opening, and cover with foil.

LOWER SHELL of tortoise is creased to suggest the joint with which a real tortoise closes its shell. The tail is modeled over a short wire bent double.

HEXAGONAL PATTERNS of twine on this tortoise's back are a realistic detail; other hexagons in the figure create a harmony of artistic qualities.

A BOY ON STILTS

This 45-inch sculpture has a simple understructure. To build a similar human figure, first cut out a coat pattern of chicken wire as you would a pattern of cloth. Tape the pieces together with masking tape. Then cut out pants and tape in place under the coat. Only the area of the shins should be visible. Cover this armature with foil and papier mache, beginning with the legs.

Make a smallish head and neck with chicken wire and attach them to the coat-torso. Cover with foil and papier mache. Build a pair of stilts, measured to the figure, using 1x1 lumber. These stilts are more than an imaginative base for the figure; they are designed to unify the figure in an original composition.

Twist, cut, and bend some pieces of chicken wire until you have roughly shaped a hand and a few inches of wrist. Jam the wrist into the

COAT PATTERN may be cut from chicken wire; cut out two sleeves (at right) and a front and a back (at left) slitting only the front piece as shown.

WINTER CLOTHING makes this figure easy to model by eliminating the need for life-like articulation, as well as producing a fresh, artistic mood.

coat sleeve and securely tape it on the inside. Make another hand and two feet, and set them in place.

Now place the figure on the stilts. Tape the hands and feet tightly to the stilts so that the connections are almost invisible. Cover the hands and feet with foil and papier mache. Improve the modeling of the hands and feet with a coat of acrylic modeling paste. This covering will also help to disguise the tape. Add shoelaces made of twine to the boots and coat them with liquid rubber latex.

Set the figure on a wooden base and nail the stilts in place. Allow the figure to tilt slightly to give the impression that it is actually balancing on the stilts. Cement the stilts to the base with epoxy resin and hide the nails with a covering of modeling paste.

Fill out the head and neck with clay and model the facial features. Cover the clay immediately with papier mache. Make a cap with window screen and papier mache. Sew a strip of cloth around the cap and the coat by adding twine dipped in polymer emulsion. Add any further embellishments you wish. Then paint the whole figure with white gesso, an arcylic primer. Use acrylic paints for the final colors. Choose colors that enhance the composition.

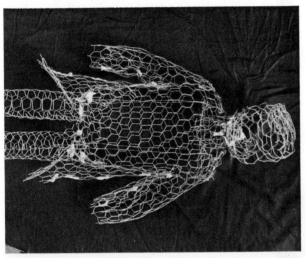

ASSEMBLE THE COAT, two cylinders for legs, and a small globe for the head, all formed from chicken wire; cover with foil and squares of papier mache.

SHAPE HANDS AND FEET with chicken wire and secure to sleeves and pantlegs. Mount the figure on stilts by hands and feet and finish with papier mache.

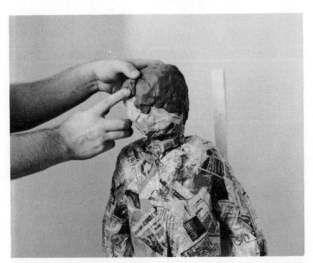

BUILD UP a thin layer of clay over the small papier mache head being careful not to unbalance the figure. Swell other areas of sculpture with clay if needed.

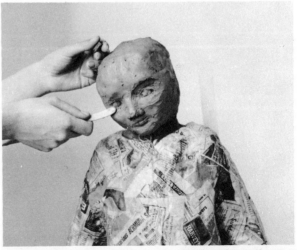

MODEL EYES and other features in the clay and cover with papier mache before the clay dries. For directions on modeling clay, see the next chapter.

MODELING WITH CLAY

Sit down with a lump of clay in front of you. Knead the clay a little. Notice how easy it is to manipulate and how its movement suggests various shapes and forms.

The qualities of clay are quite different from the other materials discussed in this book. Unlike direct plaster, its closest equivalent, clay is very responsive to precise and controlled modeling. The sculptor's hand and eye must provide that controlled, contemplative dexterity. Surfaces in clay make special demands on the sculptor, precisely because he has so much control over them. A papier mache surface grows with the construction of the figure, but no surface qualities appear in clay which are not put there by the sculptor.

Clay is normally used only for the first step in a sculptural process that leads to casting. Thus, in designing and modeling a clay figure, the eventual problems of casting must be considered. Figures can be modeled in a permanent clay substitute, but there are certain limitations, as described later.

This chapter describes the handling of clay and gives rules-of-thumb for modeling, then turns to aesthetic problems.

You will find that your success with clay does not depend as much on specialized routines, tools, and craft knowledge as it depends on your manual dexterity. The painter, Paul Klee, once remarked that the only purpose of artistic study is to acquire dexterity, so that the brain can tell the hand what to do.

TYPES OF CLAY

You can buy clay according to brand names, but in most cases the brand is of little importance. You can also purchase clay according to grade, but this is much more important to the ceramist than to the sculptor. The amateur sculptor must be sure to buy clay which has a water-base. An oil-base plasticine is not desirable.

Two different water base clays are used for the sculptures pictured in this chapter. One clay is an inexpensive 50-50 ceramic mix that can be purchased in 25-pound bags from an art supply store. The other clay, which looks different from the first clay only in color, is called Model-Light. It can also be purchased at an art supply store, for about five times the price of the ceramic mix. This clay is self-hardening, and requires no firing or casting.

Model-Light was used in five of the figures shown in this chapter: the bust, the opera singer, and the three small sketches. This permanent clay is as pliable and moves just as well as normal clay. No special instructions are needed for its use. It is especially useful and convenient for small, quickly-modeled sculptural sketches. However, small pieces of Model-Light added to a figure do not adhere well unless they are kneaded into the main surface. You must also use caution when working with Model-Light over an armature, because the clay shrinks as it dries, and may crack. This problem never arises with ordinary clay, because it is never allowed to dry.

SCULPTING A HEAD in clay from a live model is a satisfying project and will introduce you to the techniques of clay modeling discussed on pages 43-49.

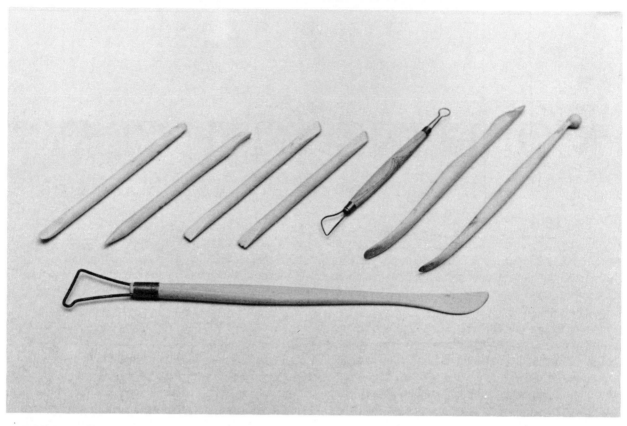

MODELING TOOLS can only supplement the human hands in working with clay. Tools such as these are not as specialized as they look; the largest tool, which combines a paddle and a carving loop, is the most useful. Common uses for the other tools are illustrated by the series of pictures shown on page 48.

Store unused clay in a covered crock or flower pot, occasionally sprinkling the clay with water. Any mould that appears on the clay can be washed away.

If you are working on a clay figure and have to leave it unfinished, cover the clay with a wet cloth. For extended delays, cover the wet cloth with a plastic bag.

TOOLS AND THEIR USE

You will find dozens of clay-working tools on display at art supply stores, though most of the tools are the same, but in different sizes and combinations. Only eight wooden tools—one 12 inches in length and the others all about 6 inches in length—were needed to model all the figures in this chapter.

Tools have one purpose: to move clay in ways that fingers cannot. Since your fingers are your most important tools, it is a good rule not to rely on other implements too much.

Flat, blade-like tools are used for an important technique called paddling. Paddling creates a surface which is smoother than a scraped or hand-flattened surface. The object of paddling is not to beat the clay into shape, but to cause it to sift and flow together, as flour sifts in a can when the can is gently tapped. Dabs of clay can be paddled into a figure without kneading and without disturbing the surrounding surface.

The 12-inch tool mentioned above has a paddle at one end, and a steel loop at the other. Looped tools, which come in many shapes, are used for moving and removing clay. In some cases, loops should also be used to whittle moist clay into shapes. In this instance, too much clay is deliberately worked into the figure, then cut away.

Other tools do not have such specific uses. They are meant to be used intuitively, for gouging, spreading, burring, or pressing the clay. The experienced sculptor usually finds a use for any tool at hand, and improvises with a pencil or a spoon if the need arises.

TECHNIQUES OF CLAY MODELING

Modeling and designing in clay are simultaneous. Therefore, the most common techniques of modeling result from habits of design, such as always working around a figure.

USE A MODEL WHEN YOU CAN

All representational sculptures begin with a model, whether it is a human body, a photograph of a sea otter, or a mental image of a shape.

Whenever possible, use a live model to sculpt a human figure. The body is too complex to be modeled from memory. With a live model your hands will be able to work spontaneously with your eye. Place your model and your figure-to-be in the same line of vision, slightly above eye level, so that you can measure one against the other without shifting your glance. Place them so that they can be turned simultaneously as you work around the figure. Proportions can be measured by sighting along your thumb. For life-size modeling, measure with calipers. Build up the rough mass of a figure at one sitting, and allow your model frequent rest periods as you proceed with final modeling.

WHEN AND HOW TO USE ARMATURES

An armature for a clay sculpture is made to support the weight of the clay, not to form contours of the figure. An armature also establishes skeletal proportions. Armatures can be omitted in sculpting small figures and figures of very compact mass.

Flexible wire for making armatures is sold in bulk, but less expensive wires and screen work equally well. The sculptured bust and the figure of an opera singer pictured in this chapter were built around armatures of chicken wire.

Ready-made and flexible armatures for human figures can be purchased in many sizes. These armatures are supported at the pelvis by a rigid, horizontal rod, and are designed for figures to be cast in plaster or metal. They cannot be used with self-hardening clay or for figures that will be cast in rubber molds.

THINGS TO KEEP IN MIND

Here are some points to keep in mind as you work from the armature stage of a sculpture to the finished figure.

1. Work evenly on the whole figure at all times. Do not finish one side or one feature before the other sides and features are proportionate.

2. Concern yourself with composition first. Realistic modeling and appropriate textures can always be handled later.

3. Also concern yourself with articulation, or the joining together of parts. The harmony of your composition and the realism of your figure depend on articulation.

4. Keep in mind the properties of whatever material you will use to cast the figure. Remember that plaster will not support its own weight in heavy extensions of form; that bronze has surface qualities which are not best exploited by butter-smooth surfaces that improve a wood carving; and that any applied texture must complement the qualities of the material used.

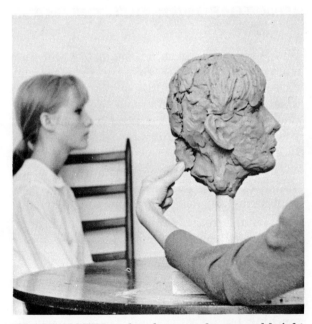

PLACE MODEL and sculpture-to-be at equal height on eye level. Have your model turn with changing posture as you work on various sides of the sculpture.

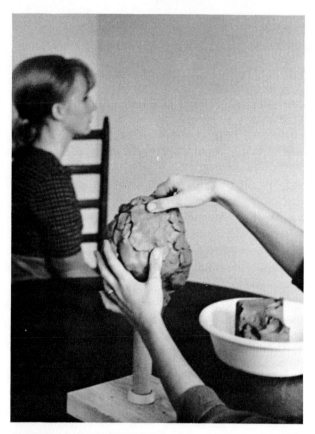

MODEL THE CONTOURS of your subject by adding lumps of clay until you have a rough mass. Work around sculpture paddling each lump to create form.

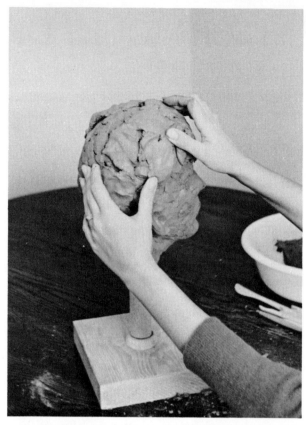

CONCERN YOURSELF with essential form first. To model a head, begin with the overall planes of the skull, add facial features, then model hair on head.

HOW TO ROUGH OUT THE MASS

With these ideas in mind, begin to build up a mass of clay over the armature. Pack the clay tightly together by adding one large lump at a time and paddling vigorously. Keep the shape rough, working out the exact proportions of your model before adding any details or any surface finish.

Three simple techniques for moving clay are presented below. One or all three of these techniques may be used in modeling your sculpture.

1. Build a mass, a feature, or a surface by adding small pieces of clay. Knead the pieces into the main mass with your fingers, or paddle with a tool.

2. Work a mass of clay by pulling and pinching. Perhaps you will instinctively work by pinching, but pinching should be used sparingly, except for very small figures.

3. Rework a mass of clay by carving and gouging with tools or fingers. Use this technique for features and surface details.

HOW TO SIMPLIFY PLANES

Simplification of surface planes is essential for the clarity of a composition. It also helps to eliminate shape-dissolving highlights and to give the sculpture a feeling of roundness and bulk.

Clay is homogeneous, while a body certainly is not. Simplification of planes is the key to suggesting the bone structures and muscle tensions that lie under the skin of your model. Thus a sculpture of simplified or abstracted planes is a more realistic sculpture.

After you have roughed out the mass of a figure, use any of the techniques described above to model the bone and muscle structure of your figure, imitating that of your model. Do not imitate exactly, but simplify the surface planes that appear in the model's features.

HOW TO CREATE FACIAL FEATURES

Complete the structure and surface planes of a figure before adding such features as the eyes, mouth, nose, and ears. Then consider the structure of the feature itself. These features can be formed in the following manner:

An Eye. First shape the boney socket, making it fairly deep. Form the eyeball by rolling a lump of clay into a ball, a proportionate size for your figure. Press this eyeball into the clay socket, but do not flatten. Form the eyelids with two crescents of clay. Place these lids on the eyeball and blend them into the surrounding skin.

Follow the same procedure for forming animal eyes.

The Mouth. A mouth is formed by the muscle structure of the jaw and the bone structure of teeth and gums. What you call the lips, or the lipstick areas of the mouth, are not separate forms, but merely patches of color on the muscles of the mouth. The surface planes of the mouth must be very simple and distinct if the lips are going to appear at all in clay.

Create a mouth by working on the whole dental area at once. The lips are two flaps of flesh over the protruding bones of this area. Two single planes separated by a little concavity form the mustache area of the upper lip. The lipstick area of the upper lip is also a single convex surface. The planes of these two lip areas intersect in a crisp and distinct line. The lower lip has the same structure, except that the convex plane of the lipstick area rolls farther over the concave plane of the underlip.

The Nose. Build the cartilaginous part of a nose only after the cheekbones, eyesockets, and nose-bridge have been modeled and articulated properly. A single, complex plane flows across each cheekbone into the bridge. The nostrils are merely a superstructure on this wrap-around plane. Where the bony bridge of the nose stops and the cartilage starts there is a break more or less visible in all noses. Below this the sides of the nose may cave in somewhat.

The Ears. The ear fits into a socket between the jawbone and the rear plate of the skull. These bones must be properly modeled in clay before any ear is attached. Then form a socket for the ear. Form a rough ear by pinching a piece of clay into the proper shape. Attach this ear to the socket, moving it around a little until it sits at the right angle. Using a looped tool, carve the ear into its final shape.

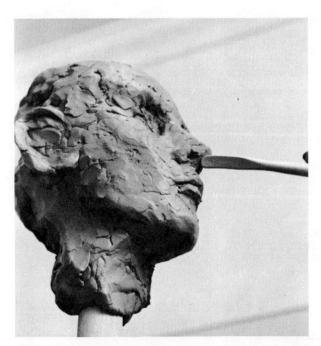

FACIAL PLANES are clear in this photograph even though surfaces have not been smoothed; jaws, cheeks, eyesockets, and forehead form a composition.

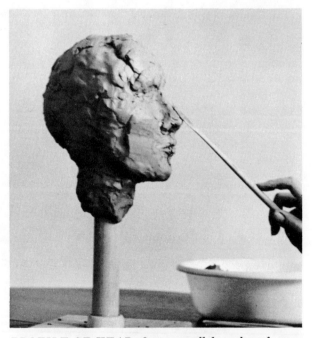

PROFILE OF HEAD shows parallel angles of composition, indicated by the slant of the tool. Creation of facial features is demonstrated by photos, page 49.

CLAY TOOLS AND THEIR USE

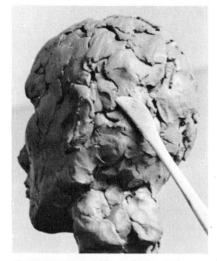

PADDLE to shift and blend clay.

SPREAD clay into smooth curves.

SLICE clay for cracks, undercuts.

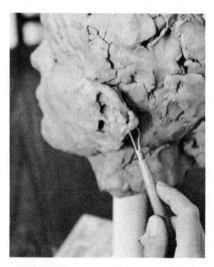

CARVE to form delicate shapes.

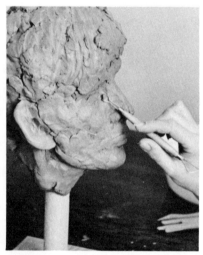

GOUGE for details and planes.

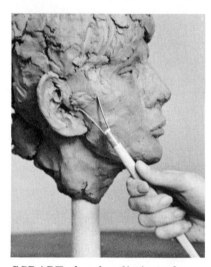

SCRAPE clay for distinct planes.

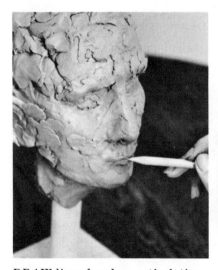

DRAW lines for clear articulation.

PROD into a clay mass for form.

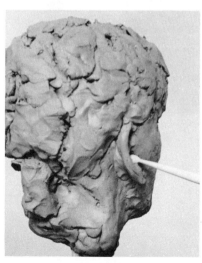

PRESS to model difficult shapes.

CREATING FACIAL FEATURES IN CLAY

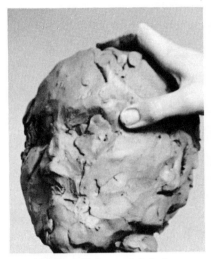

EYESOCKET *is modeled for eye.*

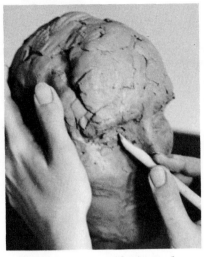

EYEBALL *is roughly formed.*

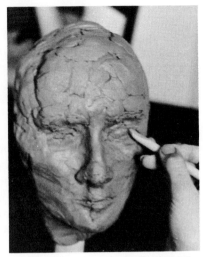

EYEBALLS *are covered with lids.*

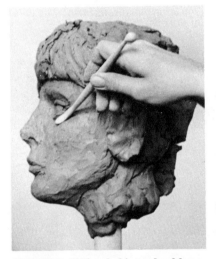

EYELID *is blended into cheekbone.*

LIPS *are convex, concave planes.*

LIPS *are clarified by modeling.*

NOSE *angle parallels head angle.*

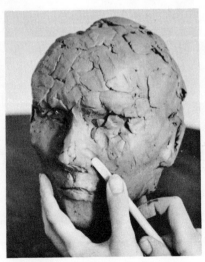

NOSE, *mouth unified by groove.*

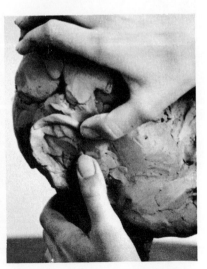

EAR *is attached, then modeled.*

SUBSTITUTES FOR CLAY

There are several substitutes for clay. Acrylic modeling paste and liquid, self-hardening metal, are inadequate for clay-like modeling. Victory Wax is a good substitute, and more durable than you might expect. Although it does not handle as easily as clay, it yields an interesting and light-diffusing surface. To make Victory Wax pliable, heat a lump of it in a gallon can or pail over a very low flame. When half of the wax has become liquid, remove it and let it cool enough to hold. Knead the remaining solid wax together with the soft wax until all is soft. Victory wax will remain workable for some time, but you cannot prepare enough and keep all of it pliable while modeling a figure. Rather than create a sculpture in batches, you may want to design your figure in clay, then copy it in wax.

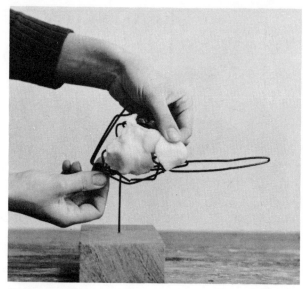

BUILD THE FORM with small dabs of soft wax pressed into a mass over an armature of wire. Wax will not shrink or crack over armature as it hardens.

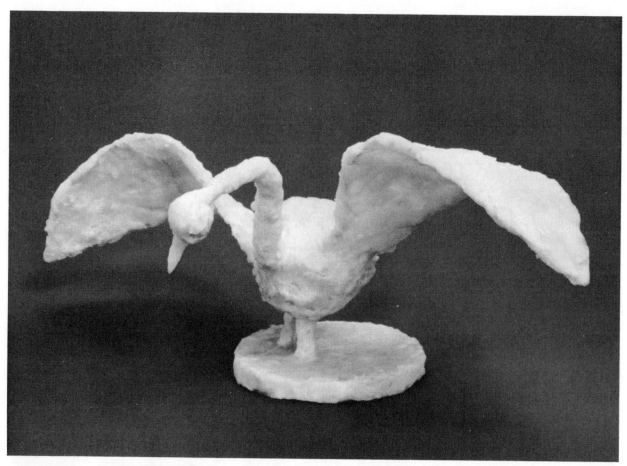

SHORE BIRD, sculpted in Victory Wax, will not be damaged by any normal room temperature. Wax has interesting colors and textures, and may be used instead of clay for modeling small figures which need no casting. For easy handling, dip your fingers lightly in linseed oil before touching wax.

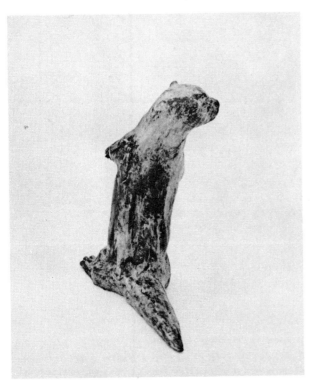

SLEEK OTTER has a form that's already simplified by nature. The model for this sketch was a photograph. You may use pictures on page 54 for model.

OPERA SINGER in a stylized costume is sculpted in self-hardening clay and glazed without a kiln by use of acrylic paints. Directions are on page 56.

BASIC DESIGN CONSIDERATIONS

The human eye does not see objects—it sees only colors. What we see as a vase is just a patch of color in front of our eyes. Nevertheless, a great sculpture stands out in the wide screen of color as an object. By means of reflected light, the surfaces we see lead our minds and eyes around and through a figure. These surfaces convince us of depth and dimensions. Perhaps we imagine that we receive a tactile impression of the sculpture. This sense may stimulate others until the sculpture seems to be more *real* than ordinary objects.

Therefore, a sculpture must impress itself upon a viewer more intensely than the object represented. This extra intensity is produced by the sculptor's imagination working through the aesthetic techniques of composition, movement of line and shape, surface qualities, and incorporation of negative space.

By now it should be obvious that designing in clay and modeling in clay are the same act. If you can comprehend how a live model is "designed," then you can model that figure in clay. Likewise, a description of how a clay sculpture is designed also tells you how to reproduce it.

The seven clay sculptures that occupy the rest of this chapter are presented both as examples of form and as projects for you to practice on. You may copy the figures, using the photographs for models, or you may simply study the forms.

The first three figures are done as sketches. A sketch can be either a small model of an intended sculpture, or an experimental model of a portion of this sculpture. Sketching not only helps you to explore and preserve an idea of design; it helps determine the best medium for your final sculpture. Self-hardening clay offers the perfect material for easy sketches.

RECLINING AND SITTING FIGURES

This sketch is an imitation of Henry Moore's style of sculpture. Considered one of the great modern sculptors, Moore is noted for experimenting with perforations. Such non-representational holes of space through a figure can lighten a figure, making shapes possible that would collapse if solid.

At the same time, perforations open up the dead space within a form and unite the surfaces by drawing the eye through the form. Most important, a perforation incorporates negative space into the sculpture. Therefore, space around a figure is unified in the same manner as the surfaces are united, creating continuity between substance and space.

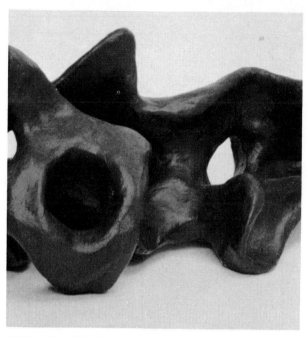

PERFORATIONS OF SPACE, visible in this Model-light sketch, help create openness of form and sense of movement characteristic of modern sculpture.

RECLINING FIGURE is modeled first by pinching and reworking a flat, oval piece of clay into a series of convex curves and waves perforated at two points.

Smooth edges and surfaces thoroughly so composition will be apparent. Form smaller sitting figure from triangular sheet of clay; glue together with epoxy.

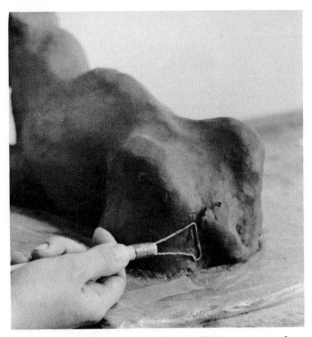

DETAILS AND SURFACE embellishments, such as the tail and tousled hair between the horns, must be added by blending bits of clay to the form.

A COW
IN SIMPLIFIED FORM

The purpose of the two abstract sketches shown on this page is to simplify the form of a cow. Both figures have been highly abstracted and reduced to their major planes. You may wish to simply copy the figures or try your hand at other ideas.

In the smaller sketch (at the right in the lower photo), no details were admitted. In the larger version (at the left in the lower photo), a decoration has been inlaid between the horns to relieve the starkness of the surface, and a tail has been added. The photo to the left illustrates how the tail flows into the ground like the rear legs and seems essential to the character of the abstraction.

SMALL SKETCH in self-hardening clay (at right) becomes the model for a larger, more detailed sculpture of cow in ordinary clay (at left) shown as rough mass ready to be smoothed and finished by paddling with tool (shown between figures). Sculpture can be cast in papier mache, following directions on page 64.

A LONG-HAIRED ANIMAL

This realistic sketch attempts to solve the problems of modeling a long-haired animal in clay without rendering the hair. The otter, with its heavy tail and sleek limbs, has an interesting form. This sketch seems especially appropriate for amplification in carved wood. The grain of the wood would compensate for the unrendered hair. It would also emphasize the compositional lines that draw together at the head. For economy of material and effort, the body and tail might be carved from two separate blocks of wood and fitted together with glue.

OTTER'S HEAD is a broad, flat box with a short muzzle; the eyes are wide-set and the ears, which are the last detail to be added, are placed at rear of skull.

MODEL TORSO and head by pinching a single lump of clay. Form legs and tail with other lumps of clay. Limbs must be attached properly to suggest joints.

STREAKY SURFACE is created by painting an uneven coat of acrylic polymer medium directly over the dry Model-light which was used to sculpt the figure.

A PLASTER POTENTATE

A minimum of shapes and planes and a maximum of surface decorations characterize this plaster potentate, marking him as a whimsical, unassuming sort. This figure was first modeled in clay over a coat hanger armature. The gown was decorated by pressing coils and squiggles of clay onto the moist mass of the figure. The completed figure was then cast in plaster. (For directions in casting a figure in plaster, see the chapter on easy casting methods.) Dry plaster was painted with acrylics in this way: the robe and base, red; the gown, orange and olive; the crown, olive; and the face, pink. Details were painted with black acrylic.

COAT HANGER ARMATURE will support a heavy, vertical mass of clay. Press bits of clay into the coils of wire; continue to add clay in dabs to finish form.

ROUGH MASS of this potentate is composed of three basic shapes, a large bell for the body, a smaller similar shape for the base, and a ball for the head.

CLAY SCROLLS pressed over the king's gown do not disguise the simplicity of this form. The figure may be cast in plaster using a rubber mold (see page 60).

AN OPERA SINGER

As simple as the figure of the king in construction, but more subtle in its spatial values, this figure was formed with Model-Light over an armature of chicken wire. This figure was created to show that surface decorations are not incompatible with formal unity. The hair, facial features, and costume decorations were cut from a rolled-out sheet of clay and then laid on the figure without being kneaded into the mass.

Some problems developed as the figure dried. Model-Light did not seem as cohesive as regular clay, so the surface decorations fell off after hardening. These pieces were simply glued back with epoxy resin. Then the figure cracked here and there over its armature. These cracks were filled with acrylic modeling paste. To hide these defects without creating distractions of color and light, the figure was brushed with a monochrome coat of acrylic burnt siena.

MODEL PROPORTIONS of this opera singer by pressing chunks of clay into the mass. Paddle whole surface smooth; attach cut-out details of clay.

ROLL OUT A SHEET of moist clay and cut out shapes with a palette knife. These shapes should harmonize with the overall contours of the figure.

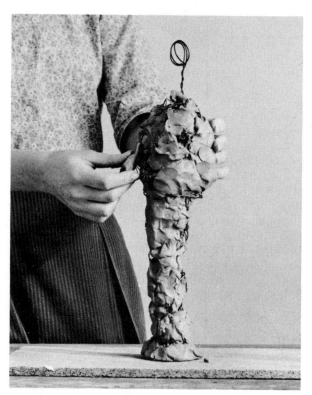

SLENDER FIGURE should be supported by an armature of wire and mesh, even though this armature may cause self-hardening clay to crack as it dries.

PRESS CUT-OUTS of clay tightly against the surface of the figure; if the shapes loosen as the Model-light dries, re-attach by gluing with epoxy resin.

FACIAL FEATURES and hair of the opera singer, and details of her costume, are created with cut-out shapes of clay, the edges of which are not rounded.

COSTUME DESIGN follows all around the blouse of the opera singer, helping to lead the eye from plane to plane, creating a sense of dimension.

FLAT SHEET of clay is the "ground"; using a pencil or a pointed tool, etch a design on a ground that is cut to the proper size for your proposed relief.

BUILD LEVELS of relief within the areas of your design by pressing dabs of clay against the ground. Create details by incising the clay with various tools.

CONTINUE MODELING with dabs of clay until all figures have reached their proper degree of relief. Relief levels should be consistent with composition.

CREATING A BAS-RELIEF IN CLAY

We have already distinguished between free-standing figures and reliefs, which are "picture" sculptures. Naturally, questions of space and continuity do not apply to reliefs, especially bas-reliefs. Composition in a bas-relief should be cast rather than sculpted in self-hardening clay or wax.

Clay reliefs should be simple in design and there should be no attempt to create great depth. Donatello and Ghiberti modeled reliefs in astonishing perspective, but few sculptors have ever equalled them. These two men worked for years on their small panels.

You will find the frieze or processional style of design easier and more natural than the

APPLY TEXTURES which emphasize the composition to the remaining flat areas of the ground. Scrape or gouge into ground for greatest variety of relief.

Renaissance style of Donatello and Ghiberti. This style of design groups figures together on one or two levels of relief against a flat ground. The relief shown on this page is a variation on the processional style of design. (This relief was cast in plaster from a plaster mold and painted with a gold patina. See page 66.) For practice, try your hand at imitating its composition, following these general directions:

Before beginning to model your relief, make a simple cartoon, or drawing, of your design. Next, roll out a ground of clay about an inch thick, trim it to the proper dimensions, and paddle the clay smooth. Then, etch the main features of your sketch on this ground.

Begin to build up the masses of the relief by adding bits of clay. When the masses are high enough in relief and clear in relationships of levels, model the details of the figures by pinching, adding, and cutting away. Complete the relief by working the whole modeled surface into the kinds of textures you desire.

FINISHED DETAIL, showing central figures of the relief, is no longer clay but cast plaster painted with a metallic patina; instructions are on page 93.

NEARLY FINISHED clay bas-relief is given final touches with a curved bladed tool. Keep relief moist until you are ready to cast it. All qualities of such a sculpture should be coherent; textures of the ground and figures should be similar to each other and should be appropriate to overall realism and perspective.

PRESERVING AND REPRODUCING FORMS BY CASTING

Although most casting methods are subtle, laborious, expensive, and messy, four relatively simple techniques for reproducing and preserving clay figures in plaster and papier mache are presented in this chapter.

Sculptors who want a figure cast in metal must search for a foundry willing and able to cast sculpture at a reasonable price. Some sculptors actually send their figures to Italy for casting.

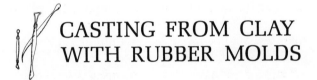

CASTING FROM CLAY WITH RUBBER MOLDS

Molds made with liquid rubber are not messy and can be made in the home. They render a perfect fingerprint impression of the clay model and can be used for dozens of castings.

A rubber mold is basically a sack with a single opening through which the casting plaster is poured and the finished figure is removed. This opening is called a mouth. Generally, molds are formed so that this mouth is at the base of the figure and thus automatically concealed. However, if the base is too small or divided into segments, there is no reason why another part of the figure cannot be the mouth. The unfinished

MANY CASTS may be made of this king from one rubber mold. Casting methods, such as described in this chapter, enable you to preserve clay sculptures.

surface left by the mouth will have to be patched with direct plaster for each casting.

The contours of a sculpture may prevent you from using a rubber mold for casting, because the entire casted figure must be pulled out of the mold through the mouth. For example, figures which have perforations, representational spaces between legs or arms, or long appendages, should be avoided until you have mastered the techniques of casting. Once you have mastered these techniques, you may wish to experiment handling figures with perforations by using shims (thin metal dividers driven into the clay figures) and mouths that can be closed and opened. Each experiment will require an individual solution.

Making a mold is almost a foolproof operation, as long as you follow the instructions exactly. Liquid rubber can be purchased at an art supply store. Just ask for latex liquid molding compound.

MOLD THICKNESS AND SIZE

Rubber molds stretch like balloons, but they don't return to their original shape if overstretched. The thicker the mold, the greater the stretching permitted.

There is no limit on the size of a rubber mold; however, an enormous mold would be hard to manage, would require quarts of latex liquid, and would require a heavy casing to maintain its contour. The sculptor would also have to have great strength to strip a very large mold from its casing.

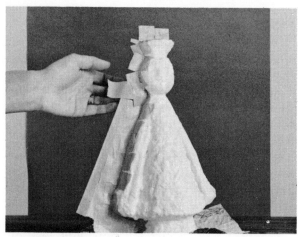

AIR-TIGHT COAT of rubber molding compound is brushed over the entire figure to be cast; paint a two-inch lip around the base for a pouring mouth.

MAKE SHIMS by cutting three-inch lengths of masking tape. Double each length so that part of it sticks together; attach each length to figure as shown.

PLACE FIGURE in a bed of paper with one partitioned area face up; coat heavily with plaster; when dry, turn figure over and form other areas of casing.

HOW TO MAKE A RUBBER MOLD

Set your clay figure on a non-porous surface. Rub a soft brush with a little soap and water and dip it in the latex compound. Paint a 2-inch circle of rubber around the base of the figure, making sure it gets on the figure as well as on the surface the figure sits on. This band anchors the mold in place and forms the mouth of the mold. Now brush a thin coat of latex over the whole figure, being careful to cover the lip around the mouth and all cracks. Allow time for the first coat to dry (but no more than 24 hours), then apply a second coat. Be careful not to make the second coat so heavy it drips.

Six applications of liquid rubber are required for a small figure; more are needed for a larger figure. For ease in removing, make the thickness of the mold as even as possible. After the last coat, let the mold cure while still on the clay figure for two days.

A MOLD CASING HOLDS THE SHAPE

Generally, all but the simplest molds require a casing. A casing is a rigid plastic jacket, made in several sections, that roughly duplicates the contours of the mold. It holds the shape of the mold while the casting material is being poured. A casing should be made in a minimum number of sections to facilitate handling.

Study your figure and determine the number of sections required. At the desired dividing lines, attach partitions made from masking tape; these will separate the sections of the casing as it is being made. Let the partitions protrude at least two inches. Paint a thin coat of cooking oil over the rubber mold, to protect it from the plaster. Now lay the figure on its side and spread fresh plaster over one section, being careful not to spread beyond the partitions. If your figure is delicate, lay it in a bed of crumpled newspapers during this process. The thickness of the plaster should be in proportion to the size of the figure.

When the first section is thoroughly dry, apply plaster to the next section. Complete the casing in this manner, leaving a thin edge of the partitions exposed all around. After all the plaster has hardened, remove the casing, section by section. If a section seems to stick to the rubber, soak that part in cold water until it loosens. Finally, gently remove the partitions.

PREPARING THE MOLD FOR CASTING

With the clay figure still inside the rubber mold, hold the mold under running water, then pat it dry with a towel. Dust the mold with talcum powder, then strip it from the clay model, turning it inside out. Again put the mold under running water to remove any bits of clay, and pat it dry. (Don't be concerned if the inside of the mold has been discolored by the clay, since this discoloration will not affect the casting plaster.) Paint the inside of the mold with a thin coat of cooking oil to prevent the cast from sticking. Turn the mold right side out and place it in the casing, tying the sections of the casing together with string.

POURING PLASTER INTO THE MOLD

Mix enough plaster to fill the mold only halfway, using three cups of dry plaster to two cups of water. Stir this mixture with your fingers until it is smooth and bubble-free. Steadily pour all the plaster into the mold. Twist and rock the encased mold until all sides are thoroughly coated, then empty the plaster.

As soon as the first shell of plaster has set up, place the encased mold in a box of sand, shredded paper, or any other material that cushions, so that the mouth points upward and is level.

To cast a solid figure, mix enough smooth and creamy plaster to *fill* the mold. Pour the plaster into the mold. Reinforce such potentially weak areas as thin limbs and necks by inserting short lengths of wire into the plaster after pouring it. Fill the mold right to the mouth, and let a little plaster brim up over the lip (this will be chipped away later). When the plaster has set up, remove the casing and strip off the mold.

Figures that have extreme contours or overhanging corners where air pockets might form must be cast hollow. Pour the mold only *half full* of plaster. Slosh it around so it covers all the sides and contours and pour out the excess. Allow time for this coating to set up, then repeat the process several times until an adequate shell of plaster is built up. Finally, stuff the shell with plaster-soaked wads of burlap cloth and fill the base of the mold solidly with plaster. Once the plaster in the base has set up, you can remove the mold. Allow several days for a plaster figure to cure before painting.

FINISHED CASING is a crude mold itself, necessary to hold the shape of rubber mold. For easy handling, make casings in two symmetrical sections.

TURN MOLD inside out as you strip it away from the clay, which may now be discarded. Wash the mold and paint it with oil before turning right side out.

SET THE MOLD mouth up inside its casing in a box of sand and pour fresh plaster into the mold in an unbroken stream to prevent air bubbles from forming.

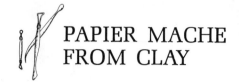

PAPIER MACHE FROM CLAY

Several papier mache casts can be made from a single clay figure. The figure becomes the actual mold over which the papier mache is cast. Such casts have the precise form of the clay model, but their surfaces will be that of papier mache, not clay. Figures to be cast in papier mache should be designed with this in mind.

APPLYING A PAPIER MACHE CAST

First coat the figure with cooking oil. Cut up a pile of newspapers or scraps of newspapers into pieces of various sizes and shapes. Following the directions given in the chapter on papier mache, dip the paper scraps in polymer emulsion and cover the whole figure, including the base, pressing the scraps tightly to the clay. Cover this skin with a coat of acrylic modeling paste. Brush this coat smooth with a paintbrush dipped frequently in water. As soon as this covering is dry, apply another skin of papier mache. If your figure is longer than 17 inches, it will require additional applications. When you have finished covering the figure, allow it to dry for 24 hours.

REMOVING THE CAST

Study the cast carefully to decide where it must be cut in sections in order to remove it from the model without bending it. Mark the cutting lines with a pencil, then cut through the skin with a razor blade. Carefully lift the sections from the model. The clay model will be of no further use for this casting. However, if you wish to use it for another casting, don't let it dry out. Start the second casting at this time. Otherwise, break the figure down entirely and store the clay for future use.

Select the least conspicuous section of the casting and put it to one side. Carefully fit the rest of the sections together and secure them together on the inside with masking tape. Take the section which you set aside and fit it into place and secure on the *outside* with tape. Coat the joints of these sections with modeling paste. When the paste is dry, cover all the joints with papier mache.

The surface of the completed cast may be decorated following any of the methods described in the chapter on papier mache.

PAPIER MACHE COW is one of several castings made from one clay model; thus it is the final version of a sculptural idea that began as a small Model-light *sketch pictured on page 53. Decorations of twine soaked in polymer medium are applied sparingly to back and forehead; sculpture is painted with acrylics.*

STEPS IN CASTING A COW

MODEL your sculpture in moist water-base clay.

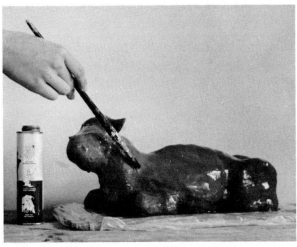

BRUSH light oil over entire figure before casting.

COVER figure with strips of polymer-soaked paper.

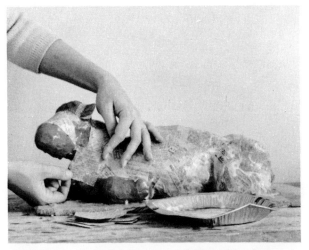

OVERLAP strips and press tightly to the figure.

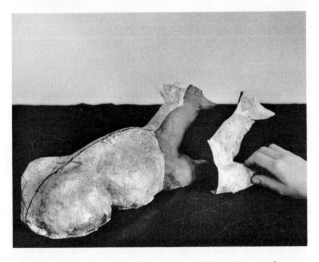

CUT casting into sections and remove from clay.

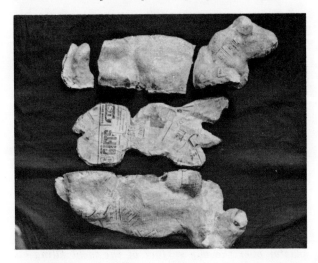

REASSEMBLE sections with tape and papier mache.

CLAY TO PLASTER TO PLASTER

This method for casting clay studies is quite simple when used for reliefs, but is extremely difficult and very messy when used for figures in the round. Therefore, this section is confined to describing the method for casting clay reliefs.

THROWING THE PLASTER MOLD

First, make a clay relief following the directions given in the chapter on clay. Place your clay relief on its back. Build walls around the relief with slabs of clay. These walls should be several inches deeper than the relief, so that they form a shallow basin.

Mix enough creamy plaster to thinly cover the model. Add a few drops of liquid blueing to the plaster and mix thoroughly. Throw or splatter handfuls of this blue plaster onto the clay relief until the surface has been covered evenly to a depth of 1/4 inch. This method of application is necessary to avoid air bubbles in the plaster.

When the blue layer has set up, mix a large batch of creamy plaster without blueing. Pour it immediately over the blue mold to a level depth of about one inch. Let this plaster harden. Remove the retaining walls and set them aside. Turn the mold over and gently pull away the clay model. Wash all traces of clay from the mold by running it under the faucet. Pat dry with a towel.

BUILD WALLS of clay around the relief and splatter blue-tinted layer of plaster over the clay surface; pour an inch of white plaster over hard blue layer.

PULL CLAY MODEL away from the hardened plaster mold; wash the mold carefully and paint it with a very thin film of light oil, called a mold release.

WITHIN CLAY WALLS, splatter a layer of white plaster over the oily surface of the mold filling all cracks. Set mesh in place and fill mold with plaster.

CHIP PLASTER MOLD away from the plaster casting (the oil film releases each piece); remove white layer for practice before chipping away blue layer.

COMIC BAS-RELIEF showing figures in a subway suggests processional style of ancient Greek sculptures and avoids problems of perspective by relying on vague, undetailed background. Directions for modeling clay relief are on pages 58 and 59. Only one casting can be made by pouring plaster into plaster mold.

POURING THE PLASTER CAST

Place the plaster mold face up (concave side up) on a bed of newspaper. Coat the entire surface of the mold with linseed oil or water-glass (available from a drug store). This coating enables you to chip the mold away from the cast. Using clay, build retaining walls around the edges of the mold, marking the top of the mold for future reference.

Mix a small batch of creamy plaster and throw or splatter it over the blue face of the mold to a depth of approximately ¼ inch. When this coating has set up, cut out a rectangle of hardware cloth, or wire screen which is slightly smaller than the relief. Place this reinforcement over the dry layers of splattered plaster. Loop two lengths of strong, flexible wire through both sides of the wire screen, a few inches below the top of the mold. These will be used to hang the finished relief.

Mix a large batch of plaster and quickly pour it into the mold, over the hardware cloth, to a level depth of 1 inch. Hold the hanging wires straight up from the mold until the plaster stiffens. Let the casting cure for a few hours.

CHIPPING THE MOLD AWAY FROM THE CAST

Turn the casting over so that the mold is on top. Using a round mallet and a chisel, chip the white layer of plaster from the mold.

Here are some hints for chipping: You must chip, not gouge. Therefore, do not hold the chisel; merely guide it with your hand. Chip downwards, perpendicular to the relief, not across it. If you can remember the contours of your relief, it will be easier to judge how much force is required for this process. Listen for a change of sound — something like a nutshell cracking — each time you tap the mallet. When you hear this, the chip is loose and may be lifted away. Also watch for tiny crack lines. Lift each piece of chipped plaster with your fingernail or the tip of the chisel. If the chisel actually chips through and touches the surface of the cast, it will leave a mark.

HOW TO MAKE A NEGATIVE CASTING

Sand or clay can be used to model and cast bas-reliefs. The same simple and direct technique is used for both materials. There is no basic model; all modeling is done in the mold itself.

MODEL THE MOLD IN SAND OR CLAY

To model a mold in sand, use slats of wood or a cut-up cardboard box to make a tray whose dimensions will be those of your relief. The sides of the tray should be approximately 3 inches high. Line the tray with plastic or aluminum foil to keep it sturdy.

Depending on how high you would like the relief to be, fill the tray accordingly with clean, fine sand. The surface of the sand must be level and be at least two inches below the rim of the tray walls. Wet the sand thoroughly and re-smooth its surface.

Model the contours of the relief directly in the wet sand, keeping in mind that a depression or incision in the sand will become an elevation or ridge in the final cast. If you have trouble visualizing these contours in reverse, make a sketch on paper with various pencil shadings or colors and study the sketch in a mirror. Undercuts and highly protruding figures are not suitable for modeling in wet sand.

To model a mold using clay, simply make a flat ground of clay and place it in a tray. Form the contours of the relief in reverse by gouging and pinching.

NEXT, POUR THE CAST

Mix a small amount of creamy plaster. Dribble the plaster gently on the wet sand (or splatter it on clay), being careful not to wash out the modeling. When the mold is covered with an inch of plaster, let this coating set up. Mix another batch of creamy plaster and pour it into the mold, following the directions given earlier in the chapter for casting plaster in plaster.

Let the plaster-filled mold set for several hours. Then lift the cast out of the sand (or pull it away from the clay). Much sand will cling to the cast. Brush off loose grains with a stiff brush; loosen other grains with a modeling or carving tool, or leave them as part of the final surface. Smooth imperfections in the finished plaster with a chisel.

SURFACE TEXTURES of this abstract relief based on Maya Indian designs reveal process by which it was modeled and cast in wet sand. Since the mold is sculpted directly, final product is a mirror image in depth of original modeling. Negative casting does not permit controlled modeling or great perspective.

STEPS IN MAKING A NEGATIVE CASTING

FILL a selected box with a level depth of sand.

WET the sand heavily so that it sticks together.

MODEL with improvised tools by gouging the sand.

DRIBBLE plaster gently on modeled sand surface.

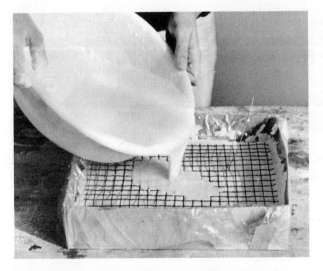

REINFORCE with mesh, pour mold full of plaster.

BRUSH the sand away from hardened plaster cast.

INCISED WOOD CARVING AND STONE SCULPTURE

Although carving in wood and stone is the most time-honored of sculptural crafts, mastery can be achieved only by patient study. Even when mastered, this craft is difficult and time-consuming, and usually requires materials which are expensive and scarce. However, most sculptors take great pains to learn carving because many design habits required for all sculptural media are derived from the disciplines required in carving.

The approach to stone and wood carving is similar only in the design problem of cutting into a rough mass to create a composition. The tools and techniques of the two crafts are different. For example, a stone such as marble cannot be cut to shape by removing large chunks. Instead, minute flakes are chipped away with special steel tools that require constant reforging. Carving a round wooden sculpture demands only whittling and chipping tools, and a practiced hand.

For the beginner, two easily mastered techniques and materials are incised wood carving (that done by furniture makers) and soft, porous stone carving. Both techniques offer equal artistic satisfactions.

Incised wood carving is recognized by the fact that designs are made by incisions in a flat surface of wood. Instead of the surface modeling that is required to gain the several levels that make sculpting in relief effective, the depth of the cuts are varied in incised carving. These cuts may form grooves, troughs with rounded or V-shape bottoms, inverted pyramids (such as distinguish chip carving), and many other variously shaped depressions. The simplest of carvings on flat panels done in this manner have a certain appeal for the very reason of their simplicity and lack of pretension.

WOODCARVING TOOLS

Woodcarving tools are chiefly sharp-edged chisels and gouges. A large array of these tools is essential if you expect to do many carvings. Otherwise, a half-dozen tools of as great variety as possible will be adequate.

The assortment of gouges pictured on the next page was used for the project that follows and combines ordinary cabinet-maker's tools with smaller tools normally used in woodcut work. The cabinet tools have shanks 5 inches long, and wood handles to be wielded by hand

FEATHERSTONE OWL is two feet high, weighs about 20 pounds. Its form was suggested by natural shape of stone from which it was carved. See page 78.

or with a mallet. The woodcut tools have 3-inch shanks and handles designed to be pushed by the ball of the hand.

You will also need a round, hardwood mallet. This round shape minimizes the chance of a tool striking a glancing blow. A pair of C-clamps may be used to hold the work steady; but it is often better to work without clamps, letting the block slide slightly or resting it against a wall or backboard.

These tools may be purchased at your local art supply store.

SHARPENING
WOODCARVING TOOLS

Carving tools must be sharp enough to shave a sliver off your finger nail. Even new tools must be sharpened before they can be used.

If tools are new or very dull, use an Indian oilstone for the first sharpening. During work, touch up the edges frequently with a hard Arkansas slip stone.

To sharpen a tool, squirt a few drops of oil on the stone. Using one hand on the gouge handle and the forefinger of the other hand to steady the blade, place the convex bevel of the blade flat on the stone. Note the angle of the handle and maintain it while sharpening. Slide the edge of the blade from side to side with a firm, even pressure. Roll the edge just enough to take in the entire curve. Do this until there is a slight, even burr on the inside edge of the gouge. Now hold the tool with this concave side pointing upward. Push the rounded edge of an Arkansas stone from side to side across the blade, using very slight pressure, until the burr is gone.

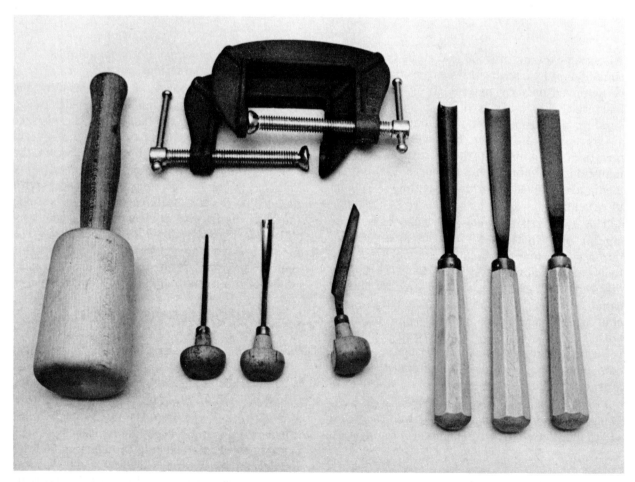

WOODCARVING TOOLS pictured here are three gouges (at right) identical except for curve of their blades, a hardwood mallet (at left), and three small tools originally made to cut wood blocks for graphic printing; C-clamps are optional accessories. Methods for using the tools are pictured on pages 75 and 76.

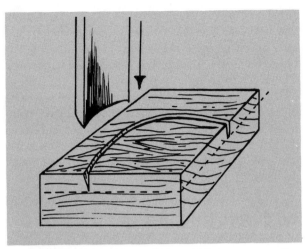

STOP CUT is made with the blade of any carving gouge driven vertically into the block of wood to exactly the desired depth of incision for your design.

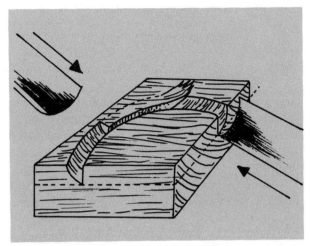

BOTH SIDES of a section of design to be left raised are delineated with series of stop cuts made with a gouge whose blade roughly matches designed curve.

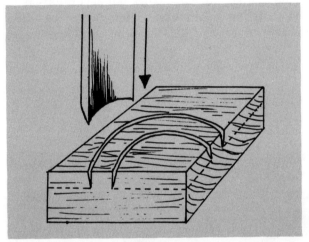

SLICING CUTS are made in combination with stop cuts to remove wood. Where a curve lies along the grain, the tool is driven with the grain as shown.

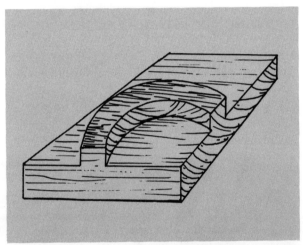

WASTE WOOD is cleaned away from both sides of raised curved section by slicing cuts, removing little chips for smoothness as bottom of cut is approached.

WOODCARVING TECHNIQUES

The grain of a piece of wood is a major factor in its appearance, and the direction of the grain must be considered when you are designing an incised carving. Medium-hard woods require little attention.

One technique, the use of "stop cuts" in combination with "slicing cuts," is so essential that it demands some explanation. The stop cut is a control cut, made straight into the wood along a line in a design where the level of relief is drawn. No wood is lifted out by a stop cut. A slicing cut is made at an angle which meets the stop cut and a chip is removed. Test your hand at making stop-and-slice cuts with each of your various tools in a scrap chunk of hardwood.

Among the useful tools for wood carving is one with a pointed wedge instead of a cutting blade. This tool should be used for engraving, or gouging, lines in wood. Hold the tool in one hand, edge and point down, as nearly level with the wood surface as possible. With an even pressure of the ball of the hand, gouge a ribbon-like strip out of the wood to form a line. This tool also may be used to clean tiny chunks and chips out of corners of your carving.

For a much more thorough discussion of carving methods and tool care, see the *Sunset Wood Carving Book.*

A HARDWOOD PANEL

An intaglio is a panel sculpture in which some features are incised while other features remain at original block-level. The techniques required for this project are simple enough even for a beginner.

For materials buy a block of finished or unfinished hardwood, at least 1 inch thick, from a lumber supply store or a cabinet-maker. (African mahogany was used for this project.) Ask for a well-cured block, neither warped nor split. Have the block cut to the size of your intended intaglio.

DRAWING AN INTAGLIO DESIGN

Before doing any carving, draw several designs on paper, choosing one that is most appropriate for development in contrasted flat areas of various depths. The main lines of composition and movement should approach or remain at the block-level, the level of the wood before incision. The level in intaglio sculpture is the equivalent of the ground, or lowest level in a relief. The block-level should spread throughout the composition for unity; therefore, do not choose a design that is concentrated in one or two figures. Work out the levels of your design with degrees of pencil shading.

EXECUTING THE DESIGN

Draw your design with pencil on the block of wood. Begin to gouge out the main areas of incision, using the combined techniques of stop cuts and slicing cuts. Work out several areas of contrasting depth first. Then carve out other areas to fit the relationships of these main levels.

Do not make all the areas flat, dead-level

PLANES AND CURVES intersect at angles in this life-size detail from the lower right corner of the intaglio sculpture, suggesting related depths and help-ing to unify the overall composition. Visible blade marks in this panel create interesting surface effect and lend unity to sculpture if handled consistently.

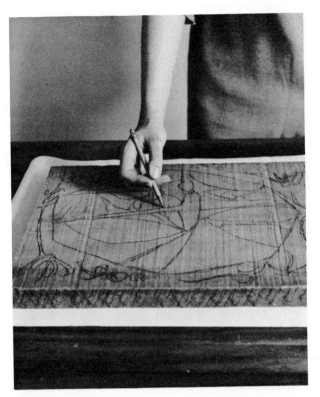

DRAW DESIGN on pre-cut hardwood block, following a sketch on paper. To make certain your design is appropriate, shade with pencil all areas to be incised.

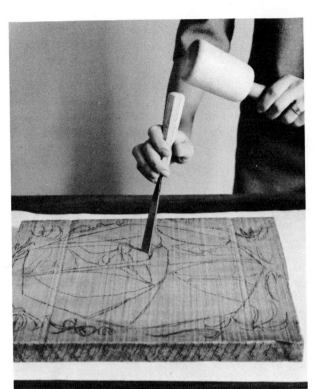

FOLLOW THE LINES you have drawn, making a series of stop cuts with any of your gouges, driving as deeply into panel as you intend to remove wood.

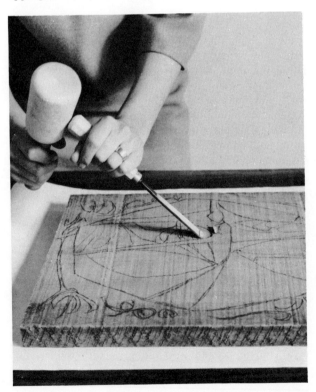

SLICE OUT chip, which should break cleanly away at the stop cut, using a gouge held at 45° angle or less and driven along the level of incision.

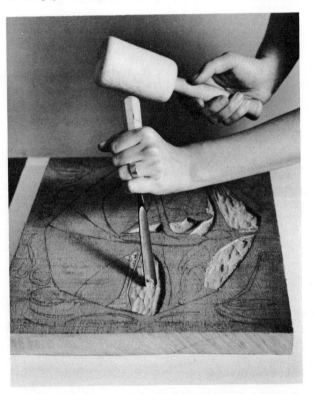

ROUGH OUT several contrasting depths in the various parts of your intaglio design to create an overall pattern of depths. (Continued on the next page.)

DRIVE GOUGE *with the ball of your right hand, as shown; and guide the gouge carefully, holding the upper part of shank very loosely in your left hand.*

WIELD MALLET *with your right hand and guide gouge with left hand, holding it loosely by handle and shank. Clear out major areas of incision in this way.*

HOLD STUBBY HANDLE *of this very sharp woodcut gouge against the ball of the hand. Use this tool to round and shape block level features and details.*

ENGRAVE LINES *and remove thin ribbons of wood with this wedge-shaped tool, wielded in same manner as woodcut tool at left. Steady block with other hand.*

depths. Consider the intaglio a matter of planes, which may intersect at angles. Study the bottom right hand corner of the intaglio shown below for an example of carving in planes. Make a stop cut along the line where two planes will intersect. Then make slicing cuts at the angle of the planes down to the stop cut.

Work out all the areas of depth and the carved planes of your design before rounding or picking out details on the main, block-level features. Use your woodcut tools to smooth out and clarify the incised areas and gouges.

Pick out details on the block-level, or non-incised, areas, using the same tools. For the final touches, round or model these areas wherever desired with fine sandpaper. You need not sand away all tool marks, since such marks often create an interesting texture.

THE FINISHING TOUCHES

Sand the uncarved surfaces of the block, including the edges. If desired, stain selected gouges and planes with a wash of turpentine and burnt umber oil paint. Then brush several coats of linseed oil over the block and drive two screw-eyes into the back of the panel for hanging.

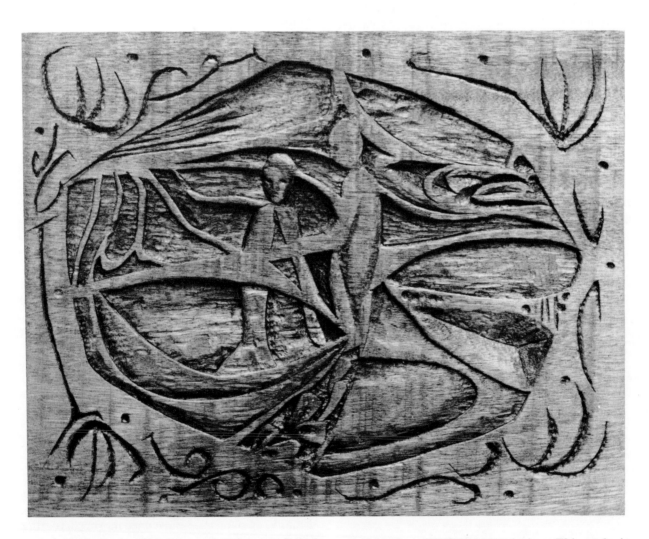

HARDWOOD INTAGLIO is made from unpolished block of African mahogany. Intaglio style is a method of carving and decision, related to the graphic artist's wood-block engraving and printing. This style involves little modeling; lines at block level create composition, and gouged out areas suggest space.

SCULPTING IN POROUS STONE

Sculpting in soft, porous stone requires fewer tools and more natural skills than sculpting in marble or granite. Neither as difficult to create nor as permanent as hard stone sculptures, the two figures pictured on these two pages may be displayed in a garden or indoors in an open area of the home.

SUGGESTED MATERIALS AND TOOLS

Soft or porous stone usually can be purchased at building supply houses, at garden supply yards, or at nurseries. Choose one that is even in consistency, is neither brittle nor crumbly, and is fairly simple and symmetrical in shape. Be sure to watch out for fissures, flaws, or other imperfections. Featherstone was used for these figures. This stone is very porous, will support its own light weight, will not chip or split as it is carved, and has an attractive gray grain.

You will need a chisel and a mallet or hammer, several large and small rasps, a small pointed file, and an old paintbrush for clearing away dust.

INDIAN HEAD SCULPTURE derives much of its design from raw shape of stone from which it was carved. Face is narrow while back of head is broad.

FIRST, ROUGH OUT THE FORM

The stone-carvings of Central American Indians suggest many ideas for designing in porous stone. Notice that the stone face shown below was designed in this style.

Rather than block out the stone and then carve deeply into it to create a pre-designed shape, allow the natural shape of the stone to determine the shape and subject of your sculpture. As with clay, design and execution will be simultaneous.

Set your stone at eye level on a protected table or working stand. Make sure there is plenty of room to move around the figure. With chisel and hammer, carefully knock off any unmanageable lumps and corners. Rub vigorously with a large, coarse rasp to smooth the stone down to its basic, essential planes and contours. Stand back and walk around to see what form the shape of the stone suggests. If no form comes to mind, decide on a simple compact subject and grind away enough of the stone with your rasp to establish the form of your composition.

Then clarify the form by scraping away parts of the stone with rasps and file. Work on the main contours before trying to carve details. Features such as nose and eyes may be left rough. Work all around the stone, as if you were liberating a real shape from a heavy crust.

MAKING THE FINAL TOUCHES

Brush off the heavy dust that clings to the figure and study it from all angles, up close and a few yards away. The contours of the figure should be clear both as a representation and as a composition. Now begin to carve features and surface details with a pointed file, using the point as well as the scraping faces. Do not seek great delicacy of modeling in such fragile stone. Finally, go over the figure once more, correcting the contours in keeping with the new features, and perfecting the surface qualities with rasps and file. No additional finishing is needed.

SCULPTING A SOFT STONE OWL

SMOOTH crude stone to essential planes and shapes.

CARVE experimentally, so that a subject emerges.

SCRAPE the stone on all sides to liberate the form.

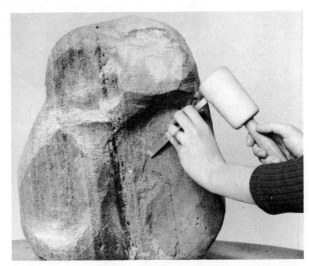

CHIP away stone to rough out the areas of detail.

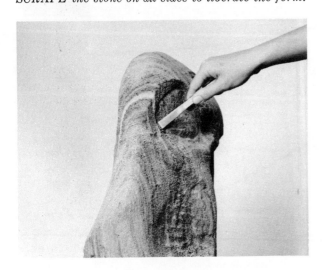

WHITTLE details with a chisel for clarity.

GOUGE into the stone to create incised details.

SCULPTURE WITH ODDS AND ENDS

Choose any materials and assemble them any way you please. This how-to rule for modern construction sculpture allows for unlimited experiments in the use of materials not originally intended for sculpture such as plywood, metal scrap, and lumber. Old furniture joints, driftwood, and even auto parts have been transformed into sculpture by imaginative artists. Sculpting in this manner is relatively a new form of art. Such constructions are neither sculptures nor paintings, but include some values of both such as composition and movement. In addition, they can often ignore or contradict traditional sculptural values.

For example, the sense of space which classical sculptors seek to achieve through various surface effects is of little importance to the sculptor of constructions. He would argue that if the human eye cannot see space, then spatial values shouldn't be an important quality of his construction. He might even build figures that seem to violate the rules of gravity, just to destroy any feeling of weight and mass.

Although construction sculptures are too individualistic to be treated with specific instructions, this chapter presents three projects which describe characteristic materials and methods for handling that may be used to create many different designs. One of the proj-

SPATIAL COMPOSITION within a confined space is created with elements of line and mass, using wire screen and plaster. Directions are on pages 85 and 86.

ects is constructed in relief. Such reliefs are uniquely flat and differ from paintings only in the use of materials and craft. This type of construction is referred to as a construction picture.

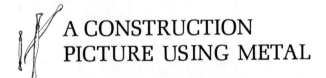

A CONSTRUCTION PICTURE USING METAL

The design of this construction picture relies on the contrasting colors and surface qualities of copper and brass for the visual interest. Instead of duplicating the design of this project, you may want to use your own imagination.

SUGGESTED MATERIALS

Sheet of plywood (18 x 20 x ½ inches)

Sheets of tooling copper and brass (2 x 2 feet)

Small copper and brass nails

Liver of sulphur (optional)

Paints

DESIGN ON PAPER OR ON METAL

Draw your own design on a sheet of paper the size of the intended background. Such a drawing is called a cartoon. Lay a sheet of carbon paper, face down, on the sheet of tooling metal. Spread your cartoon over this carbon paper and trace the design with a blunt tool, pressing evenly so that the carbon paper will reproduce the design on the metal. Using scissors for cutting copper and tin snips for cutting brass, cut out the pieces of the design.

TOOLING IS OPTIONAL

Tooling is a process of making a detailed design on a material using a sharp instrument. Although tooling is optional in building this project, it gives a nice effect for little effort. There are special tools for this process, but any clay modeling tools which have points and blades will do the job just as well.

Using a pencil, mark your tooling design on the back of the sheet of copper or brass. Remember that the design will be reversed when you turn the metal over. Place the metal on a thick pad of newspapers and trace over these lines with a pointed tool. Gouge the lines as deeply into the back of the metal as you wish them to be raised on the face.

When the design has been deeply engraved, turn the sheet of metal over and lay it face up on the pad of newspapers. Rub the non-raised areas of the design with a bladed tool. The metal will become stiffer and tougher as it is rubbed.

If copper has been used as the tooling metal, it may be darkened with a brushing of a solution of liver of sulphur. Small chunks of this chemical are available for purchase at most drugstores. Pulverize the chunk and dissolve a

TOOLED COPPER, discolored with liver of sulphur, is contrasted with unpolished tooled brass and plywood painted with gold patina (see page 93) to give depth and visual interest to finished construction picture from which this detail is taken. Tooling design fills up copper pieces to suggest mass and movement.

A CONSTRUCTION PICTURE—SIX STEPS

ENGRAVE lines in the back of cut-out tooling metal.

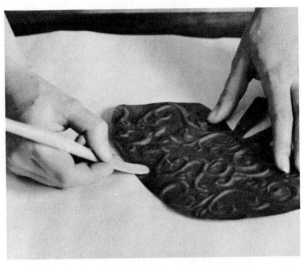

RUB flat areas around lines on front of the metal.

PAINT liver of sulphur solution on tooled pieces.

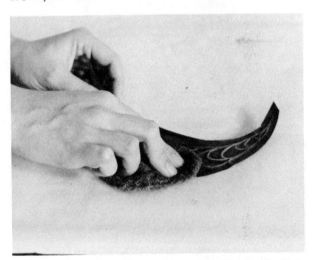

POLISH the blackened pieces with fine steel wool.

SPREAD pieces of metal on cartoon, checking design.

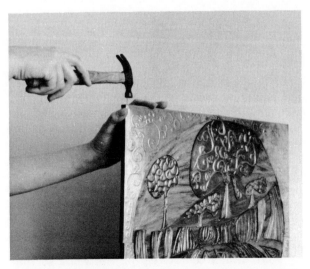

ASSEMBLE pieces and nail to the plywood ground.

FINISHED CONSTRUCTION is a semi-abstract landscape in which simple tooling is used to portray leaves and branches on the trees, grass on the row of *copper squares in middle ground, and waves on rippled shapes in foreground. No special tools needed for this sculpture; instructions apply to any design.*

teaspoon of the powder in a pint jar full of water. Brush this solution evenly over the pieces of copper and let stand until the copper has turned the desired shade of darkness. Rinse off the pieces of copper with water and wipe dry. Using steel wool, polish the raised areas of the tooling and any other areas where you wish the copper color to shine through.

ASSEMBLING THE PIECES

Make any necessary adjustments in design and then cut the sheet of plywood to the desired dimensions for your background. Lay the pieces of your design tentatively on the wood so that you can decide what part this background will

play in your final sculpture. If the background is going to be entirely covered with metal, then it need not be finished. Otherwise, any part of this wooden surface that shows must harmonize with the color of the metal surface. One way to accomplish this is to paint the plywood with gold lacquer, and then brush parts of it with an oil wash of burnt umber.

Lay the metal pieces in place on the finished background. When you are completely satisfied with the design, secure the individual pieces, using copper nails on copper pieces and brass nails on brass. Scatter the nails around the pieces, not just on the edges, so that they do not form a definite pattern which will unbalance your composition.

A CONSTRUCTION
IN A CONFINED SPACE

This simple abstract construction within an open frame may be used as a space divider in a room, or as an elegant space filler in a bookcase. Constructions also can be created in closed frames or boxes. Either way the space confined by the frame becomes negative space, or space that is part of the sculpture.

SUGGESTED MATERIALS

Two finished redwood boards (3 x 1 x 14 inches)

Two finished redwood boards (3 x 1 x 20 inches)

Epoxy resin

Nails

Sheet of window screen (1½ foot square)

Five 36-inch aluminum straight wires (fairly heavy gauge)

One 36-inch aluminum wire (thinner gauge)

Plaster

Flat black spray paint

Varnish

COMPOSING THE CONSTRUCTION

Approach this sculpture not as a project to be built but as a problem to be solved. The problem is that you have a large, shallow square of empty space. This space must be cut up with interesting lines and partially filled with interesting shapes. A harmonious composition of space and materials must be created.

Assemble the four redwood boards into a rectangular frame. Coat the joints with epoxy resin and nail the frame together. Square the corners carefully and allow the resin to harden.

Begin to cut up the enclosed space, using the five heavy aluminum wires one at a time. You

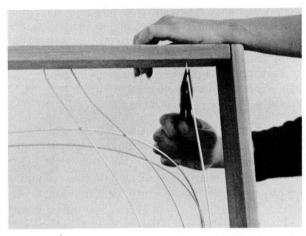

INSERT TIPS of aluminum wires in the inside walls of a rigid wooden frame, using wires to cut up the enclosed space and to create compositional movement.

BEND PIECES of window screen over tiny frames of wire and add these shapes singly or in clusters to the composition of wires and space within the frame.

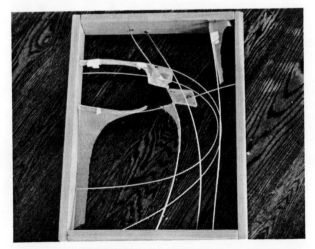

ATTACH SHAPES to wires with masking tape or thread, working each into design without overcrowding given space; when design is finished, apply solder.

need not use the full lengths of each wire. Set each wire in place by drilling a small hole in the inside wall of the frame as needed. Continue to add wires until your composition begins to have proportion and movement. One at a time, remove the end of each wire, dab the ends with epoxy resin, and reinsert into the frame.

Cut the sheet of window screen into pieces of various sizes and shapes. Begin adding these pieces to your composition, keeping within the lines of movement created by the wires. Try to create a center of interest with a cluster of shapes, but do not allow this center of interest to overwhelm the wires and space. Temporarily fasten the pieces of screen to the wires with little bits of thread. When all of the pieces of screen are in place, dab each joint with glue or heatless solder. When the glue has hardened, mix a cup of creamy plaster and spread it heavily over the pieces of window screen.

Now cut the thinner aluminum wire into two or three lengths, and bend these short lengths into squiggles and spirals. Use one bent wire to break up the space at the center of interest, harmonizing the plaster shapes with the stiff compositional wires. Use the other wires to emphasize the most important movements in the composition. Tie these detail wires to the fixed wires wherever they touch. Cover the tied joints with epoxy resin or heatless solder.

THE FINISHING TOUCHES

Mask the wooden frame with newspapers and spray the wires, pieces of screen, and plaster with flat black paint. Apply several coats of this paint, allowing each coat to dry thoroughly before applying the next. Remove the newspapers and sand the frame. Then paint the frame with clear varnish.

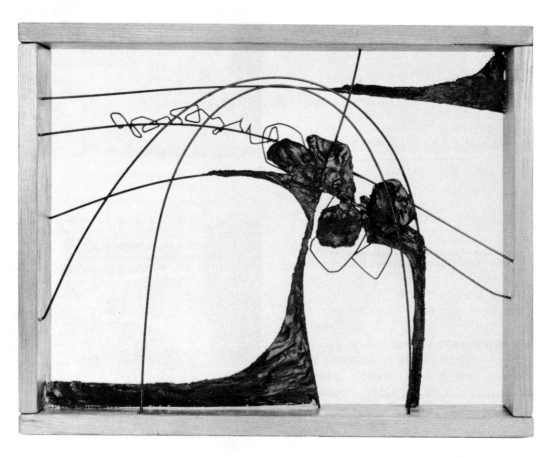

VERSATILE CONSTRUCTION may be turned on any side (see page 80) and displayed as a hanging, room divider, or space filler in a bookcase. Some of the wires and plaster-coated shapes protrude slightly from frame; others recede into it. Design and assembly proceed together; each step suggests next step.

A FREE-STANDING WOOD CONSTRUCTION

Three feet high and five feet long, this construction contains 50 separately prepared blocks of redwood and pine. It is the most ambitious project presented in this book. You may design and build a similar composition by following the general procedure presented below.

SUGGESTED MATERIALS

Block of finished redwood 2 x 12, 4 feet long

Block of finished redwood, 2 x 4, 3 feet long

Block of clear redwood 2 x 2, 10 feet long

Block of clear redwood, 1 x 1, 10 feet long

Redwood half-round, 1 inch, 5 feet long

(Other soft woods may be substituted for redwood throughout)

1½-inch pine closet rod, 3 feet long

1-inch pine closet rod, 3 feet long

1½-inch wooden closet rod socket

Scrap of sheet metal, 2 foot square

Three aluminum wires of medium gauge, or several feet of another stiff wire

Nails

Two tubes of epoxy resin

Masking tape

Linseed oil

SKETCHING AND PLANNING THE DESIGN

This construction began as a sketch, that is, an experimental assembly of 6 redwood blocks built to test a visual idea. The idea was to fix many blocks of wood together, building a seemingly weightless sculpture that would visually burst with suspended motion. The initial sketch was incorporated into the final sculpture.

The general composition of the figure was planned before any pieces were assembled. As the figure was executed, the designed composition developed as follows: A center of interest was created near the larger of two supporting poles. Lines of motion radiated from this center, which eventually became a dense cluster of pointed blocks. One major branch was created to give the impression of toppling backward from the center over the smaller supporting pole, becoming less energetic the farther it extended. Smaller branches reaching in other directions were used to counterbalance this long branch.

SUGGESTED TOOLS

Keyhole saw or jigsaw

Metal hacksaw

Four-sided wood rasp

Triangular file

Hammer

Pliers

Tinsnips

Wire cutter

Drill and bits

Sandpaper

C-clamps of various sizes

Paint brushes

HOW TO PREPARE THE BASE

When similar plans have been made for your construction, prepare a base by carefully sanding the 4-foot length of 2 x 12-inch redwood. Drive a heavy nail into the center of the block, 10 inches from one end. Cut the head off the nail with a wire cutter. Cut and sand a 10-inch length of 1-inch closet rod. Coat one end of this rod with epoxy resin, and drive this end down onto the headless nail. Make sure the rod stands perpendicular to the block. Thirteen inches from the other end of the block, center the 1½-inch wooden socket and glue it down. Nail in place, leaving half the nail protruding. Cut off

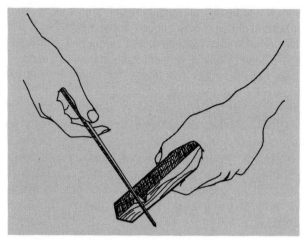

SCORE WOODEN BLOCK with file or rasp at an angle calculated to be joined with an edge or a scored niche in another block. Score deeply for strong joints.

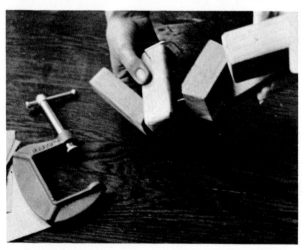

FIT BLOCKS together in a balanced series of five or six, chosen for variety and movement. Secure joints with nails and epoxy resin. Construct several series.

JAGGED CLUSTER of blocks, forming a center of interest and of weight, is mounted directly on the main support pole and braced with masking tape.

the nail head. Cut and sand a 13-inch length of 1½-inch closet rod. Coat the socket and one end of this rod with epoxy resin. Drive the rod onto the nail in the socket, making sure it stands completely upright. Allow the resin to thoroughly harden overnight.

HOW TO PREPARE WOOD ELEMENTS

Saw about half of the redwood and pine boards into blocks of various shapes and sizes up to eleven inches in length. Sand the surfaces of each block, rounding some corners and edges, and squaring others. Prepare additional blocks only as needed while constructing the figure.

ASSEMBLE ELEMENTS INTO SECTIONS

Select several blocks to form one section of your sculpture. Begin with a section that will rest on top of one supporting pole. Hold the blocks up to each other at various angles until the arrangement pleases you. Using the flat side of your rasp, score the surfaces of the blocks, wherever two blocks are to be joined. Have as much surface touching between blocks as possible for strong joints.

To join two blocks, drive a nail half way into the scored surface of one block and cut off the nail head. Coat this surface and that of another block with epoxy resin. Force the coated surface of the second block over the headless nail into a tight bond with the first block. Tape the blocks in place, or fix them in a C-clamp.

In this same manner, join the remaining blocks into sections. Limit each section to essential blocks, those that carry forward the main lines of the composition from one to another. Details may be added after the overall figure is complete. Set each section aside until the glue dries, but do not remove the tape.

ADDING WIRE AND SHEET METAL

Wire and sheet metal scraps should be added to the various sections before they are mounted in the main body of the composition. Cut out pieces of sheet metal with tin snips, and file the edges smooth. Using a thin-bladed hacksaw, cut a gash in the wooden block where each metal piece is supposed to fit. Coat with epoxy resin the areas of the metal piece that will fit into the gash and tape in place until the resin hardens. Use such pieces sparingly. In this construction only one metal piece serves to connect one block to another.

Wire can be used to emphasize and expand the shapes and angles of important blocks, somewhat as a shadow emphasizes a figure. Cut a length of wire and bend it to fit around a block. Each end of the wire must be long enough to jab into the block. Drill holes in the block the same size as the wire. Dab the ends of the wire with epoxy resin and insert into the holes.

JOINING THE SECTIONS

Join the end blocks of finished sections with nails and glue. Begin by securing one section to the end of one supporting pole. Brace this section with a stack of books. In the same manner, join a section to the other pole. Use tape liberally for support. Then connect the sections

that will be placed between the two supporting poles. Allow the glue on all joints of these sections to harden; then remove tape and braces.

Assemble the sections of the other branches. Join and mount the sections one at a time, starting with the most central. Use plenty of tape and braces.

FINAL FINISHING DETAILS

When the primary structure is completed, remove all remaining braces and tape. Study the composition, and add blocks of wood wherever necessary, using epoxy resin to form the joints. Secure the blocks with tape until the resin hardens.

Remove the last bits of tape and sand away any stains on the base. Paint the whole construction with four coats of linseed oil. Paint the wires and sheet metal pieces with brownish red oil color.

REDWOOD AND PINE construction defies the laws of gravity through the use of epoxy resin and strategically placed nails. Fifty blocks of wood connected to each other at odd angles flow gracefully over two thin supporting poles. Pieces of wire and cut-out sheet metal shapes add textural interest to sculpture.

SURFACE EFFECTS OF PAINTS AND PATINAS

Many people are startled to learn that ancient Greek sculptures were once brightly painted, and that the austere, white marbles of the Renaissance period were sculpted in mistaken imitation of such classical figures whose colors had worn off. Many sculptors still ignore the possibilities of painting a sculpture because they feel that colors are not compatible with pure sculptural surface values. This is true for materials with beautiful and durable surfaces, such as stone and bronze. However, papier mache, plaster, wood, and clay all require special treatment to preserve and improve their surface qualities.

OIL PAINTS ARE TRICKY BUT FUN

Oil colors often are not consistent in their intensity, and because of this are difficult to mix to a desired hue. Purples and greens are especially hard to produce by mixing. Even mixing together any of the several reds, blues, and yellows, may produce an unpredictable shade, usually muddy and dull. The addition of

THREE STAGES are involved in painting this papier mache bird (see page 34): seal surface with varnish, spray with black lacquer, decorate with oils.

black or white may also diminish the intensity of a color drastically.

For the beginner, it is best to invest in a wide selection of prepared colors, and learn by experience to modify colors to the exact hue desired.

Oil paints can be used on almost any surface, including all the materials in this book. However, a plaster surface must be primed with wall paint or spray paint before an oil will cover it well. Without a primer, plaster will respond more easily to acrylic paints (discussed on the next page).

Good oil paints are thick and homogeneous, and remain workable on the palette for hours. They also take hours to dry. Oil paints can be thinned with linseed oil or with turpentine. Thinning does not make oils easier to use; therefore, colors should be thinned only when a special effect of paint is demanded.

Oil paints are sold in art stores, hobby shops, and even variety stores. Many brands are low-grade colors. The most intense and reliable colors are made by two companies, Winsor-Newton and Grumbacher.

WASHES GIVE SPECIAL EFFECTS

Washes are used to bring out sculptured textures and to create surface highlights. To make a wash, dilute a dab of oil paint with turpentine to any desired consistency. Then brush the wash over a surface with the surface face pointing up to the ceiling if possible. This will allow the wash to run evenly over the figure and settle in any cracks and depressions. Use a rag to blot any excess amount of wash that may settle.

HOW TO MAKE
OIL PAINTS TRANSPARENT

Transparent colors applied over each other produce interesting surface effects. There are two ways of making oils transparent. One method is to thin a color with turpentine and brush it very lightly over another dry color. The second method is to mix an oil color with turpentine and damar varnish in any proportions. Brush this color over a dry surface in coats of any thickness. The transparency will be luminous and the surface will have a glazed effect.

With either method, but especially with the second, you must build up a backlog of experience in order to control the relationships of your colors. A transparent color painted over another bright color may yield an unpredictable third color.

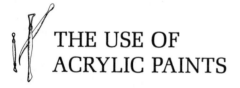

THE USE OF
ACRYLIC PAINTS

Acrylic paints contain microscopic bits of colored resin suspended rather than dissolved in a polymer emulsion which ensures their stability and permanence. They are sold under several labels in art supply stores, hobby shops, and even discount department stores. Acrylic colors dry quickly.

Because acrylics are manufactured in fewer hues than oil, mixing of colors is likely to be required. However, unlike oils, acrylics are nearly uniform in intensity and lend themselves to easier blending.

Acrylics are sold in both jars and tubes, the jar colors being thinner in consistency than the tube colors. Both types of color are perfectly opaque if used without thinning.

HOW TO MIX COLORS

A minimal array of acrylic colors that can be mixed for most sculptural purposes are cadmium red, cadmium yellow, alizarin red, diaxazone purple, phthalocyanine blue, phthalocyanine green, burnt umber, red oxide, and yellow oxide. The cadmium colors mix well with each other to produce various shades of orange. The phthalocyanines combine easily to produce lucid shades of blues and greens. Alizarin blends well with phthalocyanine blue to produce a spectrum of blues and purples. The last three colors are earth colors, that is, warm natural colors which are impossible to produce by mixing and which do not mix well with other colors. Painted on a pure white surface, all of these colors will be bright and clear. On a colored surface, they may be cloudy and dark, in which case titanium white may be added to lighten them. Titanium white and mars black may be mixed, at the cost of some intensity, with any color to produce pastel and gray shades. However, experimentally, add white and black in small dabs, because they may transform a mixed color into an unexpected shade of brown.

THIN ACRYLICS FOR TRANSPARENCY

To make acrylic colors more or less transparent, you may thin them with water or polymer emulsions. Washes of any consistency and gloss also can be produced by thinning acrylic colors with water or acrylic emulsions. Thinned with much water, these colors act like ordinary water colors, but are more durable when dry. Tube colors mixed with polymer gel will retain their consistency but will dry less rapidly and will be somewhat transparent. Polymer medium may also be used to thin an acrylic tube color to the exact consistency of jar colors, but the color will then be very transparent. In general, use jar colors for easy handling and for direct painting with non-transparent color. Use tube colors for impasto (heavily painted surfaces) and for a wide range of transparent effects.

To achieve extraordinary transparencies and glazes, mix any acrylic color with polymer emulsion and apply directly over other dry colors. The more emulsion included in the mixture, the more transparent the color will be. Then apply a coat of straight polymer emulsion to increase the gloss.

USE GESSO AS A PRIMER

Acrylics will not bind directly to a metallic or oily surface, but if a white acrylic primer, called gesso, is applied first, it will produce an ideal ground for acrylic colors. A transparent color painted over a dry coat of white gesso will produce a luminous, lightened hue. This technique frequently results in better and lighter colors than would be produced if the same color were mixed with white before application to an unprimed surface.

Used very heavily, acrylic paints will help to smooth out irregularities of a surface. Additional smoothing may be done by sanding the paint itself.

METAL PATINAS GIVE SPECIAL EFFECTS

Many fine lacquers are sold at hobby shops in metallic colors such as gold, copper, and bronze; but these lacquers are imperfect for sculptural purposes because they imitate only the fresh color of the metal, not its characteristic discolorations. A realistic metal patina can be created only by painting a metallic lacquer over or under a coat of acrylic or oil paint that has been mixed to match the metal's oxide.

MAKING A COPPER PATINA

Copper becomes green or black when weathered. To imitate this stain on plaster or any other surface, first coat the surface with gesso, a white acrylic primer. Then paint it smoothly with copper lacquer. When this is dry, discolor it with a watery wash of dull green. Brush the wash heavily over some of the surface and lightly over those areas where real metal would retain its sheen through polishing.

MAKING A GOLD PATINA

Since gold tarnishes rather than discolors, no paint will mimic the beauty of gold very well. However, the use of gold lacquer brushed lightly over a wash of red oxide or burnt umber, or

vice versa, will produce an interesting patina. If the surface to be painted is dark, apply a primer coat of gesso.

MAKING A BRONZE PATINA

Bronze comes in many hues and weathers in various ways. Light olive green brushed over brass or bronze lacquer will imitate one typical bronze color. Raw umber washed over gold will suggest another. To achieve a fine bronze patina, prime the surface with gesso. Brush the surface with raw umber, darkened by mixing a speck of black; let this dry, then brush over it heavily with bronze lacquer. A finishing touch for this patina is to brush it with a wash of green to imitate the green oxide that gathers on a bronze statue that has been exposed to rain.

THE NATURAL FINISH OF WOOD

Although Medieval woodcarvings were brightly painted, the natural color and grain of wood is more beautiful and renders a better sculptural effect. This is especially true when the grain of the wood is harmonious with the composition. In order to preserve wood finishes, they must be sealed. This can be done by using any of the following products:

Linseed oil can be painted on wood with a soft brush, and then rubbed to a sheen, if possible. Additional fresh oil must be applied to this surface occasionally. Regular butcher's wax also produces a good sheen. This wax must be rubbed into the wood with your fingers.

Varnish on wood sculpture produces a highly protective finish. Paint two even coats of a very clear varnish over a figure that has been carefully sanded. To create a recently excavated look, sand across the grain of the wood and paint with a heavy dark varnish.

Staining of a wood that is pale and unattractive can be useful before sealing it with linseed oil or wax. A thin wash of burnt umber oil paint mixed with turpentine will produce a reddish stain. The stain can be rubbed on the wood with a rag or with a pad of steel wool.

MEXICAN STYLE CANDELABRA is constructed like a direct plaster sculpture by wrapping strips of plaster-soaked cloth around tubes of chicken wire.

INCISED CARVING will add interest to bare boards of a wall whether inside or outside. Major lines are cut with gouges and details are colorfully decorated.

GARDEN SCULPTURE is created by modeling concrete mixed with asbestos and vermiculite over armature of wooden blocks and wire mesh forming shape.

CONCRETE PANEL with glass inserts is cast in a mold made by modeling right in sand bed. For panel displayed indoors, use plaster instead of concrete.

BRIGHT-EYED BIRDS are attached to stakes and can be moved easily. Bodies made from pieces of sheet copper soldered together; wings and tail are wire.

POTTERY WIND BELL is really an abstracted form of a bear adapted from an Indian design. Designs made entirely with sheets of clay must be kiln fired.

BAS-RELIEF is constructed with cut-out shapes of plywood and hardboard glued and nailed to a plywood ground, then painted with coats of white lacquer.

REINDEER AND SLEIGH are carved in white, floating soap with a paring knife. Soap may be used to create festive decorations or sculptural sketches.

INDEX

All projects are listed below in *italic* type.